Gardens

Gardens

ARCHITECTURAL DIGEST

Edited by Paige Rense
EDITOR-IN-CHIEF, ARCHITECTURAL DIGEST

The Knapp Press
PUBLISHERS
LOS ANGELES

Copyright © 1983 by Knapp Communications Corporation

Published by The Knapp Press
5900 Wilshire Boulevard, Los Angeles, California 90036

Library of Congress Cataloging in Publication Data

Main entry under title:

Gardens: Architectural digest.

    1. Gardens—Design—Addresses, essays, lectures.
2. Gardens—Addresses, essays, lectures. I. Rense,
Paige. II. Architectural digest (Los Angeles, Calif. : 1925)
SB472.4.G37 1983   712   83–211
ISBN 0–89535–117–X

Printed and bound in the United States of America

10 9 8 7 6 5 4 3 2

CONTENTS

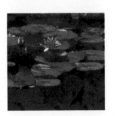

FOREWORD

"**I** CAME TO LOVE MY ROWS," Thoreau said of his Walden garden. "They attached me to the earth, and so I got strength." There is a strength to be derived from gardens, one that warms the spirit and enchants the eye, even when the garden is not of our making.

In selecting the subjects for this book, we have assembled a round-the-world and round-the-year diversity of designs. Representative of many cultures and tastes, some are fine in their discipline and restraint, others are splendid in unfettered grandeur.

While some are the work of noted landscape architects of this and other centuries, an astonishing number represent the flowering of nonprofessional talents. But all, in the process of evolvement, had the cooperation of that greatest of landscape designers, Nature, with her unerring sense of color, her skillful manipulation of form. The results of these mutual endeavors are presented in seven categories: English, Classical, Oriental, Country, Estate, Exotic, and Special.

Anyone who has ever looked into the pixie faces of a bed of pansies, or touched the magic "spring" that makes a snapdragon snap, suspects that Nature may have a sense of humor. There can be no more enchanting illustration of this than "A Green Menagerie on Narragansett Bay," where the art of topiary, with Nature's cooperation, has shaped trees and shrubs into such enchanting forms as camels, giraffes, swans, bears and donkeys.

Because winter is often overlooked in relation to beauty in the garden, we have included "A Winter Garden in Bucks County," where the lyric lines of leafless trees amid white landscapes project images that rival the most luxuriant of summerscapes.

The great eighteenth-century landscape designer Capability Brown, the originator of the English "park" style, is relatively unknown by his given name of Lancelot. He is known by his nickname, which derived from his habit of commenting, when viewing a garden he was to redesign, "Ah, yes, it has great capabilities."

There spoke the gardener. He knew the secret of landscape artistry—revealing that all gardens have great capabilities.

We don't have to garden, in order to appreciate them, any more than we must be artists, to enjoy art. For readers who are avid gardeners, this book will inspire creativity; it will be equally rewarding to those who prefer to experience nature visually.

—Paige Rense

INTRODUCTION

A GARDEN IS A LUXURY available in every part of the habitable world and on every scale, from Versailles to a window box. Nowhere can it be purchased ready-made. To create and maintain a garden requires not only imagination but a lasting will. In his way the gardener is an artist, but his art is unique. Paint a picture, and it may be finished within weeks; it should survive indefinitely without retouching. Compose a poem or a piece of music, and it can be printed or performed centuries later, just as you intended it. But a gardener's work is never complete, and in his eyes, however it may appear to others, it is never quite without blemish. Conversely—and happily—the gardener can always improve upon his patch of land.

No garden since Eden has been "natural." Nature does not create gardens. It collaborates with man by supplying materials. Some, like rock, soil, and flowing water, are helpfully eternal. Others, like plants and trees, constantly grow and change. The gardener's task is to transform what nature provides into something that appears to him delightful. He shifts things around to "improve" on nature, and introduces design where none existed.

Each garden expresses a particular concept, a personal variation on a theme dictated partly by tradition, partly by geography and climate, but mainly by the owner's idea of what a garden means to him. All gardens begin with a plan somewhat determined by what is there already—slopes, water, cragginess, buildings, trees. Very often the accidents of site dictate what the gardener adds. Unless he be Louis XIV, he cannot drastically remold ground to suit his design. But if the existing contours suggest the basic shape, much can be done to elaborate upon it with walls and hedges, by incorporating or planting woodland, by judicious garden architecture—steps and terraces, statues and pools—creating in fact a series of stages for the seasonal performances of the plants. Every garden shows a different response to similar opportunities, but almost all have two motives in common: to create surprises within a confined space, and to serve as a transition between the home and the world beyond it.

The grandest gardens ever constructed, those of France and Italy, in the seventeenth and eighteenth centuries, were designed to arouse astonishment more than surprise. At Vaux-le-Vicomte or Caserta, everything could be seen from the windows of the saloon, and if you toured the garden, it would not be on foot examining, but in a carriage surveying. There was scarcely a flower in sight, but much ornamental architecture and huge symmetrical pools with fountains awed the viewer. The purpose was to demonstrate affluence and the power to impose order upon a huge portion of a vast landscape. Today such displays awaken our historical curiosity, but what tends to delight us far more is the combination of expectation and surprise, the expectation that there is always something more to be found in a garden, and the surprise of finding it.

Gardens have ways of keeping their secrets in reserve, and foremost among them is careful subdivision, a principle that can almost always be applied. Such a garden is divided into a succession of parts—a chain of smaller gardens—with a firm design uniting them into a whole. Imagine all walls between a row of individual gardens behind a city street suddenly removed. The result would be chaotic. The unity of a garden is achieved by tempting glimpses of one part from another, by entrances that entice but do not reveal, by paths that lead and steps that wind, by swiftly flowing water that connects one section to another, by statues, pavilions and isolated trees that signal from a distance, by groves that gently divide.

All such gardens have been designed from the start from the point of view of the stranger walking through them when they have reached maturity. He will need no guide because the paths and vistas will be sufficient to direct his footsteps, and he will alternately be exhilarated and amused, falling for the tricks the gardener has cleverly contrived: a magnolia suddenly flaring to treetop height; a stream cascading over a miniature precipice; or an enclosed space, suddenly discovered, filled with flowers of a single hue.

Yet each type of garden offers its special delights. A classical garden seduces first by its geometry, its jigsaw pieces interlocked but with the joints still visible, in a pleasing combination of shapes and patterns. There is a subtle blending of textures—stone, water, grass, pebbles, boxwood, yew and cypress. The surprises come from the particular way the elements mesh, and the pleasure they give from showing that, within limits, man can control the waywardness of living things.

At the opposite end of the spectrum are gardens offering a wholly different concept of refinement. Here the purpose is not to demonstrate human control over a wilderness but to enhance it by helping nature reveal itself to best advantage. Man's intrusion is deliberately concealed. The suggestion is that nature has performed a little miracle without human help, but on a smaller scale. Where there are forests in the wild, we have in these gardens carefully sited single trees. Instead of lakes, there are pools. Instead of rivers, streams. Instead of massive cliffs to be clambered over, short slopes and meandering trails beckon. Wild flowers may be scattered across a natural landscape, but in gardens like these, it is more likely to find a concentration of them in such variety as to defy probability, but not belief. The garden is a tribute to the wilderness that surrounds it, and the sequence of surprises is such as nature itself might offer.

How well gardeners have rung the changes on these themes—from those that begin in opulent imitation of Versailles and happily melt into the free-flowing naturalism of surrounding pools and woodland, to those where the symmetry of flowerbeds and borders is softened by the tumbling exuberance of floral color. These are ways to blend regularity with romanticism. Let azaleas blaze at a distance like a forest fire, and for a few weeks in the year you will have a startling exclamation point.

Most gardens, however, unless self-contained as a city garden must be and Oriental gardens are by tradition, borrow from the surrounding landscape for their grandest effects. It can be something as neighborly as the spire of a village church seen over a garden wall, or as wide-ranging as a glimpse of another country, across a bay. At times a garden is a mere tightening of the landscape, a slice of Earth made private and habitable, as in the eighteenth century, when dukes employed Capability Brown to design scores of square miles to form an effective backdrop for their Palladian mansions.

In truth a garden has no other purpose than to act as an extension of the dwelling. It is an enticement to go outside, just as the house should be a magnet to draw you back within. They are complementary, and need to be in sympathy. The noted landscape designer Edwin Lutyens created his garden paths and placed his benches to encourage the continuation of a conversation begun indoors. The paths were just wide enough for two people to walk side by side, and outdoor stairs were spaced in easy treads so that the strollers would not be distracted by the descent.

Marriage of house and garden can be contrived by garden doors and French windows, by outdoor eating places or a belvedere for more adventurous alfresco repasts, by trelliswork and climbing plants against the walls. But most important, there should be a general consonance of scale between the house and garden. There must be mutual harmony. The view of the garden from the house must be as pleasing as the reverse.

The gardener needs, of course, to anticipate the appearance of his handiwork in all seasons. For some the flowering season is distressingly short and the plantsman's dream too briefly realized, but still the garden must not be an eyesore when moribund or dead.

Some are, indeed, at their best in winter when blanketed by drifts of snow. Then an occasional early bloom brings a world of pleasure. Others are most beautiful when flaming with autumn's colors.

Is there a danger that the world's gardens will come to have too great a sameness because every plant is available everywhere and every shape and style of garden has already been tried out in every country? As in every other art, wholly novel variations on an old theme seem impossible until one is discovered. No, I suspect inventiveness is as strong as ever, and that stagnation in garden design is as unlikely as it is in growing plants. The truly conservative gardens, unchanged for centuries, are the Chinese and Japanese, which incorporate subtle religious themes. In the West there is constant experimenting. Such attempts broaden our knowledge of what will grow where, by transporting lovely specimens from the obscurity of their natural habitat to places where they can be examined, enjoyed, and introduced like welcome strangers to flourish alongside the indigenous plant population. Has this not been the purpose of flower gardening throughout the ages?

In their different ways all gardens are outdoor exhibitions. The flowering plants of a herbaceous border are like pictures on the walls of a gallery, to be examined as you walk by, and a topiary menagerie suggests an open-air display of sculpture. All are diversions for a promenade, places to walk in and through, briskly toward a viewpoint or slowly in contemplation over carefully spaced stones. Though they are places with still centers, gardens are associated more with movement than repose, for we have decided—have we not?—that the most magical gardens are those that offer the visitor a series of related discoveries. One of the Persian words for garden was paradise, and it did not mean stillness. It meant the sort of excitement generated by love, in other words exhilaration, of which one form is surely the joy of seeing beautiful things in open air.

—Nigel Nicolson

Gardens

PART ONE

English Gardens

"England may justifiably take pride in her roses and her history, and this charmed plot has more than its measure of both."

ELIZABETH LAMBERT

ORDER AND DISORDER; the wall contains, the rose climbs over; the path is straight, the violet seeds itself in every chink—the art of the English garden is in taking care to make it all look less manicured. Gardeners have come to a harmonious agreement with nature and have faced up to the mists and temperate air that get things off to a good start, but soon encourage unruly behavior in plants. Gentle jasmine runs riot, and ivy has been known to creep into cellars, loosen corks and drink whole bottles of port. Faced with such vigor, the gardener can only call the inevitable an asset and try to put some order into all that green.

Centuries of experience help. The English garden progressed from intricate patterns in the seventeenth century to superb parkland designs in the eighteenth century and an unsurpassed interest in plants during the Victorian age. The patterns came with the Restoration, when Charles II returned from France full of enthusiasm for the formality of Le Nôtre. The great landscape gardens were the pastoral scenes that developed after William Kent had "leaped the fence, and saw that all nature was a garden," in the words of Horace Walpole. The Victorians brought rare plants from the far corners of their Empire and set them in stiff ranks, creating work for many gardeners. Since then William Robinson rediscovered the wild, Gertrude Jekyll invented the herbaceous border and Vita Sackville-West showed how to divide a large garden into smaller "rooms."

The boxwood hedges that once made patterns now give structure to the flowers, which are allowed to drift and generally behave as nature intended. Gardeners number plants among their best friends and consider that looking after them is half the fun. It may happen that on a day when the sun shines and bees hum they *might* be content to sit and take tea midst the roses, but they probably would rather be sorting out the wayward ivy. They plan for the gray months by planting boxwood and yew as geometry for all seasons, then annually add flowers for a haze of color—a formal plan, informal planting, then let the flowers have their way.

Bampton Manor
in Oxfordshire

In one of the garden's graceful borders, plants skillfully mingled for color and form suggest daubs of pigment on an artist's palette.

COUNTESS PEGGY MÜNSTER'S herbaceous borders at *Bampton Manor,* in Oxfordshire, are said to be among the best in all of England. And so they are, for she is a superb colorist and has a genius for blending flowers as though they were fresh watercolors. The countess began gardening at *Schloss Wasserleonburg* in Austria, her first home after she married, and continued wherever she and her husband lived. All the while, she collected plant names as others might gather tubes of paint, and her palette was full when she and the count moved to Bampton Manor in 1948.

There she found the flatness of the Thames valley, the hues of Cotswold stone and the intimate feeling of a walled five-acre garden, where the only reference to the world beyond it is the beautiful fifteenth-century spire of the village church next door. It was a fine starting point, but she also felt the need to create vistas within the sequestered space. A long allée of yew hedge was already established. One hundred and five feet long, it leads in ceremonial splendor to the front entrance of the manor house, now enhanced by the countess's famed double herbaceous borders. With this promenade as her point of departure, the countess proceeded to define the garden with two other roomlike enclosures, one round and one square. In each of them, yew hedges make a solid background against which the colors and shapes of flowers play.

If the borders afford a lovely background for strolling, the round garden, across the lawn, is the ideal spot for sitting quietly. Twin weeping pear trees guard the entrances to this hideaway where, within dark green walls, all is white and silver. On again across the lawn to the third "room," a square herb garden where soft grays form the base for a froth of pink standard roses. The plants read like a herbalist's dream: apple mint, thyme, golden oregano, pink and blue lavender, marjoram, purple sage.

Surrounding these three garden "rooms" are other vistas, composed of pleached lime trees, beds of iris edged with lavender, and old-fashioned shrub roses. Where once there was a paddock for a pony, the countess has put a pond, its banks planted with a willow that seems to weep into the water. Amid these many delights, the seasons pass with loving hands. Ineffably gentle is the progression of colors and forms with which the countess has brought her art to delicate perfection at Bampton Manor.

A glory of color proclaims the deft hand of Countess Peggy Münster at Bampton Manor, in Oxfordshire. A highly acclaimed feature of her walled garden is the pair of herbaceous borders that edge a grass path leading to the manor house. Low plants—including speedwell, pinks and yarrow—grow closest to the path, while taller species, like peonies, roses and delphiniums, are banked behind.

ABOVE: *Within the intimate walled garden, the 15th-century spire of the village church, Saint Mary's, provides a solitary reminder of the world beyond.*

LEFT: *A hedge of clipped yew embraces a secluded circular garden planted only with white and silver flowers. Among this delicate medley are iceberg roses, tall, bell-shaped campanula and daisies.*

RIGHT: *The silvery gray leaves of artemisia are a foil for other plants and for a swath of pebbled paving in one of the garden's more open areas.*

BELOW: *The massive yew hedges that now bound the 105-foot-long herbaceous borders were already an established allée when the countess and her husband acquired the estate in 1948. The hedges' effectiveness as a background inspired her to enclose other areas of the garden in like manner.*

Situated near the stable house is a roomlike enclosure, a square herb garden outlined by a hedge of yew. Plants here are carefully chosen for color and uniform height, with standard roses rising above. Rue, pink and blue lavender and apple mint are among the misty low-growing plants disposed in L-shaped beds at the corners of this garden. Golden and silver thyme surround the sundial; "Time against thyme," says the countess whimsically.

To replace a paddock, the countess devised a shallow pond to vary the vistas within the garden. Water lilies float upon its glassy surface, shaded by a weeping willow tree. Hostas and ornamental grasses gently cluster at the water's edge.

The Garden House in Devon

A special strain of azure poppy grows luxuriantly large in this congenial setting at the edge of Devon's wind- and rain-swept Dartmoor.

THE GARDEN HOUSE, near Buckland Monachorum, in Devon, is situated on the western edge of Dartmoor, a rocky, windswept plateau. Much of each year cold rain drenches the land. Mists linger in the low-lying areas; craggy outcrops are sculpted into strange forms, and hawthorn trees grow twisted in the severe weather.

It seems an unlikely place for a garden called "the most beautiful acre in all of England." Yet there it is, hidden in a valley and tucked behind a Medieval stone wall twelve feet high. The entrance is a Gothic archway fitted with a massive oak door. The latch is heavy and hard to lift, and the door creaks open slowly. Inside, unexpected and as breathtaking as a brilliant fireworks display, flower beds glow with color in a dozen separate little gardens. A grassy path leads through the flower beds to another Gothic archway on the garden's far side. In the middle of the garden, the path passes between a thatched stone barn festooned with climbing vines, and an ancient tower with sedum, button ferns and harebells growing from its many crevices.

Although the structures infuse the landscape with a Medieval atmosphere, The Garden House is of recent origin—conceived in 1945 by Mr. and Mrs. Lionel S. Fortescue. Mr. Fortescue started gardening while he was a teacher of languages at Eton College. When he and his wife, Katharine, decided upon an early retirement, they searched for a suitable site for their dream garden. The former vicarage of Buckland Monachorum appealed to them, though when they first saw it, the enclosure was just an overgrown orchard.

The most striking aspect of the Fortescues' garden is its richness of color and the enormous size of its plants. Indeed, the garden seems inhabited by a supernatural presence that protects the flowers and assists their profuse blooming. Perhaps it is the spirit of an old abbot who lived and died here after the dissolution of Buckland Abbey by King Henry VIII in 1536; or perhaps it is gnomes adding their sprightly presence. Four decades are hardly a long time in the life of a garden, yet the plantings at The Garden House appear to have been there forever. No doubt the loving care the Fortescues lavished upon their personal park contributes to this effect. And, though neither ghost nor goblin has ever been glimpsed among the shrubs and flowers, some friendly force does seem to be at work.

For centuries an English vicarage, from 1945 on The Garden House represented a dream fulfilled for the late Lionel S. Fortescue and his wife, Katharine. Beside the path that traverses the garden, and ensconced among the shrubs and flowers, stands a stalwart thatch-roofed stone barn, probably built in the 14th century.

LEFT: *Casting a mood of mystery over the entire garden is an ancient tower, the crumbling remains of the original vicarage. A net of color ensnares the ruin, seen through a veil of* Rodgersia; *dwarf bellflowers cling to the old stonework. A granite staircase ascends through the interior to a doorway that opens onto a high secluded garden.*

BELOW: *The massive oak seat in the hidden garden above the tower seems a primeval relic on the velvet lawn.*

ABOVE: *An age-old stone wall cloaked in wisteria and climbing roses shelters the lower garden—an inviting potpourri of color and fragrance.*

LEFT: *A total contrast to the brilliantly colored flower beds are shady passageways formed by tall hedges of Leyland cypress. These narrow corridors connect different parts of the garden and offer protection from the winds that sweep into the valley from cold Dartmoor.*

Great Dixter of Sussex

Plants flourish in the appropriately named Long Border. An outstanding feature of the gardens, it is seventy yards long and five yards deep.

I N 1910, WHEN MY FATHER acquired *Great Dixter,* in Sussex, where I now live, it was advertised simply as "an agricultural property with farmhouse attached." There was no garden, just an orchard, a wild pear tree, a fig, a bay laurel and a solitary yew. All these remain today. Yet the manor of Dixter was mentioned in the *Domesday Book,* and the sturdy half-timbered hall was built around 1460.

Dixter was a case of love at first sight for my parents, and they engaged Sir Edwin Lutyens not only to restore and add to the house but to plan the layout of the garden as well. I was born there and I have never wanted to live anywhere else. All my writings about gardening have had this well-loved place as their mainspring.

I enjoy the firm design that links all the elements at Dixter— the oasthouse, barn and other farm buildings, with the house itself presiding benignly at the center. But my chief interest has always been in plants and the clothing for this lovely framework. It was my mother's passion also. She it was who turned the many areas of rough grass into meadow gardens. To the tapestry of wild flowers she added others, and I have added more still.

The mixed borders of many kinds of plants—shrubs, annuals, bulbs, hardy or tender—are what have brought the gardens at Dixter their fame. There almost seems to be a yeast at work among the plants, so that they rise in folds, flow out onto the paths in pools of color, interlock and embrace.

As to plants, I suppose the most important feature is the Long Border. Backed by a yew hedge, it is seventy yards long, five yards deep. The path along its front margin is longer still—110 yards, ending in a loggia at its lower end, and with a delightfully simple oak seat, designed by Lutyens, at the top. Immediately on the other side of the path, past a strip of mown grass, follows the ebullient abandon of the orchard. Here snowdrops and crocuses in earliest spring are followed by daffodils in alternating drifts of yellow and white. After them, a festival of wild flowers.

The cry today is for labor-saving gardening, but gardening deserves time and effort, and I can think of no more satisfying rewards than those it has to give. And it is a healing occupation. If you have troubles, you can dig them in.

Famed English architect Sir Edwin Lutyens originally conceived the framework linking the gardens of Great Dixter, in Sussex. Lutyens also restored the 15th-century house, built of Wealden forest oaks, for the parents of horticulturist and author Christopher Lloyd; they acquired the property in 1910.

A terrace at one end of the Long Border virtually overflows with two types of roses, Irish Elegance and Albéric Barbier. Both bushes, as old as the garden, were planted about 1912.

Circular steps designed by Lutyens link the terrace near the house with the Meadow Garden and an old orchard. A type of Mexican daisy has sown itself over the years among the step risers.

LEFT: *Among the farm buildings at Great Dixter is the tiled Sussex barn, circa 1450. Campanulas color the quadrangular Barn Garden, which frames a sunken garden designed by Mr. Lloyd's father, Nathaniel.*

RIGHT: *Water lilies brighten the surfaces of several ponds on the property. Situated along the approach to Great Dixter is the Horse Pond, originally excavated for iron ore. Later, the pond provided water for farm horses.*

BELOW: *Near the Barn Garden is the oasthouse, once used for drying hops. Roses, dianthus and ballota bask near a capped brick wall with archway, designed by Lutyens.*

A Cottage Garden in London

A view from the residence shows the enclosed garden to be divided into three parts: paving, closest to the house; next, a lawn bordered with flowers; and beyond a small pergola, a wild woodland garden.

NELL GWYNNE LIVED HERE in the seventeenth century. Architect Peter Silsby's flowers now thrive in the London soil that was her vineyard, but for anyone of a romantic turn of mind there's more than roses in his garden. Think of it. "Pretty, witty Nelly"— orange seller, actress, favorite mistress of Charles II—might have walked right here, new slippers of satin and lace upon her tiny feet. A century after Nell and her king were gone, the waters next to Nell's house were found to be medicinal. These were the days of the Regency, when all of liverish London society was making its way to Bath. What luck then to find the waters closer to home. The area was renamed Spa Fields, with Bagnigge Wells Tea Gardens *the* place to visit. Crowds came: for the afternoon, for the "season," and some stayed in the late-Regency houses that were built over the vineyard. It is in one of these residences that Peter Silsby now lives.

When he moved in, the garden was derelict, so Mr. Silsby began with the spade, only to have it stop with "a spine-juddering shock." He had struck rock. All over the eighty-by-twenty-foot plot, slabs of stone covered those renowned wells. He covered the slabs with soil, took out several old vine stumps, and began again on what he calls his "cottage garden," replete with peonies, campanulas and roses—of course, roses. Nearest the house, Mr. Silsby used brick walls and stone paving in a somewhat square shape. The rest of the garden is given over to a lawn bordered with flowers, and beyond that a pergola leads to a wooded and slightly wild glade.

Mr. Silsby carefully plotted groups of color and contrasts of foliage and texture, but friends began giving him cuttings of this and bulbs of that. A few seeds came on the wind as well, and soon things settled comfortably into the higgledy-piggledy. Now if a shrub sprawls so that he cannot mow the lawn under it, he simply gives the plant its own floor of paving stones instead.

Tranquillity reigns in Peter Silsby's garden. French doors open from his living room onto a raised terrace where tea is set on summer afternoons. Here are the country pleasures of London. England may justifiably take pride in her roses and her history; this charmed plot has more than its measure of both.

In London, on the site where Nell Gwynne's vineyard flourished in the 17th century, architect Peter Silsby has devised a luxuriant setting in the cottage garden tradition. A wide border near the house is planted with cinquefoil, campanula, bush morning glory, climbing roses, buddleia and peonies. Walls enclosing the garden create a temperate microclimate favorable to relatively tender plants.

OPPOSITE: *Roses, lupine and campanula contribute most of the color in the garden. Tucked away in the background, practically hidden under a canopy of leaves, is the little pergola Peter Silsby designed.* ABOVE: *Roses planted in a line across the garden lend a sense of geometry. Within this framework campanulas, lupines and alyssums seed themselves lavishly, producing a characteristic free-form effect.*

23

Barnsley House
in Cotswold Country

Foxgloves are the dignified star of one of the splendid herbaceous flower beds at Barnsley House.

T HIS IS ENGLAND'S Cotswold Country, where sheep stand like rock outcroppings and villages have names like Lower Swell. *Barnsley House,* situated on the old Roman road, is far easier to find than Rosemary Verey, who lives there, for she is out in the garden by eight every morning, then tucked away later in the day writing about other people's gardens.

For many years only grass covered the Vereys' 3½ acres. When David Verey inherited the house in 1951, the children pleaded for a cricket pitch, a croquet lawn and a paddock, so the family grassed over the existing flower beds. Then, as a gift one year, her children gave Mrs. Verey a membership in the Royal Horticultural Society and a blank notebook labeled "Your Gardening Book." Clearly it was time to do something about the garden—but where to start?

Fortunately, Mr. Verey presented his wife with Russell Page's book *Education of a Gardener.* She took advice and courage from its pages and eventually carved out crosswalks and vistas, tunnels and focal points across the garden. As her confidence grew, she edited colors to shades of yellow and pale mauve, with lime green foliage.

Mr. Verey inherited some architectural books, and his wife became curious about the quotations in them from early garden writers and herbalists. She was determined to find those old horticultural tomes, and with luck, persistence and much time spent at auction houses, she succeeded. Today her library dates back to 1551. As her thoughts filled with the plantings of the past, Mrs. Verey's garden soon filled with them, too. Now knot gardens, inspired by sixteenth-century models, contrast with formal parterres and clipped allées based on seventeenth-century designs. There is a "wilderness" of ornamental trees in the eighteenth-century style, and enough rare plants to satisfy the most avid nineteenth-century collector.

A stroll through the garden becomes a journey through the centuries. Mrs. Verey delights in the idea that people have lived on this spot for thousands of years. She relishes the image of Romans marching past, of the fourth-century inhabitants whose relics were found nearby, and takes special pleasure in the knowledge that this land has been well cared for since the house was built, in 1697. Rosemary Verey joyfully carries on that tradition. Though at one time she may have been unsure about how to begin her garden, today she is never at a loss about how to continue it.

Soft colors and long vistas are among the delights of Rosemary Verey's 3½-acre garden in Gloucestershire. Loose plantings of lupine, mullein, box honeysuckle and campanula form a misty contrast to the Cotswold stone house built in 1697.

A stone path is all but hidden by a tumble of rockroses and lady's mantle. Irish yews flank this walk, which illustrates Mrs. Verey's love of dramatic vistas.

ABOVE: *In one of four symmetrical flower beds, a swath of lady's mantle introduces Iceberg and Rosemary roses, mingled with foxglove, delphinium, campanula and fragrant mock orange.*

LEFT: *The mixture of herbaceous plants in another flower bed reflects the predominant colors of the garden. Rosemary Verey favors yellows, pale mauves and lime green.*

Set against the dark and stately forms of evergreen cypress trees, the delicate blossoms and curving branches of a Yoshino flowering cherry tree create a particularly graceful pattern.

Beyond a water-lily pond and an aureate display of primroses and monkey flowers, Georgian wrought-iron gates add a sense of enclosure to one of the most effective tableaux in the garden.

Villa Gamberaia in Florence

Climbing roses entwine an antique stone dog that perches on a wall overlooking a vast panorama of the city.

THE PAST LIVES ON in Florence, in the art and the buildings, in the look of the surrounding hills studded with vineyards and olive orchards. Nearby, in the tiny village of Settignano, the *Villa Gamberaia* and its garden also retain, to a remarkable degree, their original flavor. Though time has wrought its changes, the present owner, Dr. Marcello Marchi, has returned the garden to its eighteenth-century design, carefully restoring the characteristics of traditional Italian landscaping.

Architects during the Italian Renaissance believed that the garden of a country estate should serve as a transitional zone between the structural regularity of the house and the irregular lines of the countryside around it. They also felt that as a visual extension of the house, intended to be lived in, the garden should be composed of different roomlike areas. Such thinking governs the plan of the Gamberaia's garden. Clustered on the small, irregular hillside plot are a formal parterre, a sunny bowling green, a cool grotto and, on the level above them, a shady ilex grove, a cutting garden and a lemon house. Thus the transition is made, in stages, from the villa to the surrounding landscape.

The American author Edith Wharton visited here around the turn of the century. In *Italian Villas and Their Gardens,* she wrote that, among the Florentine country estates, the garden of the Villa Gamberaia not only possessed "to an unusual degree the flavor of the past," but was also "probably the most perfect example of the art of producing a great effect on a small scale." She admired the relationship of the simple Tuscan villa, built by Zanobi Lapi around 1610, to its elaborate traditional garden, laid out by the wealthy Capponi family in the following century.

A procession of owners altered the garden somewhat over the years, and it was probably during World War II that the Gamberaia's fate was most severely imperiled. When Dr. Marchi acquired the property, shortly after the war, both villa and garden were in a state of near ruin. The house had been gutted by fire, the ponds desiccated; the paths were weedridden, and the evergreen shrubberies had grown shaggy from long neglect. In the years that followed, Dr. Marchi patiently restored the garden to its former beauty. Today, cherished and meticulously tended, the Gamberaia again evokes the exquisite order and serenity of the old Italian garden.

Restored to classic perfection by its present owner, Dr. Marcello Marchi, the Gamberaia, in Settignano, is a preeminent example of an old Italian garden. The elaborate geometry of the water garden makes an effective foil for the simple lines of the Tuscan villa, built in the early 17th-century by Zanobi Lapi. Near the foot of the garden, the semicircular water lily pond caps a procession of symmetrical pools.

The art of topiary is practiced with extraordinary skill and precision in the parterred water garden. Here boxwood, cypress and yew, stone and water are the basic ingredients that maintain the garden's beauty independent of the seasons. The terminal arcade provides a sense of containment; its archways, frames for the spectacular view of Florence. Set off by lemon trees, the long greensward at left is the bowling green.

An occasional element defies the meticulous symmetry of the water garden. The most whimsical touch is a single enormous sphere, here glimpsed through an arch in the terminal arcade. Overgrown and neglected when Dr. Marchi took charge, the area now recalls the carefully tended state of the villa's landscape at the turn of the century.

ABOVE: *Azalea and rhododendron blossoms add their ephemeral color to the small grotto, a traditional feature of the old Italian garden. From this cool and sheltered sanctuary, double balustraded stairways ascend to the shady ilex grove, the cutting garden and the lemon house, where citrus trees are kept in winter.*

LEFT: *A statue adorns a niche in the grotto's rough wall of tufa stone, softened by a cascade of wisteria.*

The Tuscan Villa La Pietra

A terraced path, bordered by hydrangeas, leads to the central section of the garden. Interlacing branches compose a natural arch.

T HE VISITOR TO THE garden of *La Pietra,* only a mile from Bologna, is amazed to learn that it was laid out by my father, Arthur Acton, in 1904. In fact, antique drawings prove that a formal garden existed here in the fifteenth century, but it vanished, like so many others, in the nineteenth-century craze for so-called English gardens. My father re-created it as he supposed it might have been originally. Enough traces of the fifteenth-century design remained for an imaginative reconstruction.

Francesco Sassetti, an enlightened banking partner of the Medici, purchased the property in 1460. In 1546 his descendants sold it to Giuliano Capponi, son of Piero, the Florentine patriot who retorted to French King Charles VIII's threat to sound his trumpets: "If you sound your trumpets, we shall ring our bells." It remained in the Capponi family for three centuries, until my parents purchased it from one of their collateral descendants.

From the rear façade of the house, with a view toward Fiesole and the blue hills near Vallombrosa, the garden descends in a series of terraces. The first level is a platform with a stone balustrade for statues at regular intervals; the lower terrace is sheltered by low walls with niches for other statues. Centered on this and the lowest terrace are graceful fountains with water lilies and goldfish, surrounded by stone benches and plots of grass inside hedges of clipped boxwood. The terraces are planted mainly with evergreens, so it is a garden for all seasons, independent of fading flowers.

Paths running parallel to the hillside lead to stone arches and circular plots enclosed by cypress hedges and allegorical statues. Sunlight and shade are as carefully distributed as the fountains, terraces and statues, which include a colossus signed by Orazio Marinali (1643–1720) and the vivacious figures in the open-air theater, works of the eighteenth-century Venetian Francesco Bonazza.

Though so near the city, the garden is an oasis of peace, a sanctuary for crested hoopoes and amorous nightingales. On June nights it is illuminated by flickering fireflies; the air is crystalline. The surrounding vineyards protect it from modern encroachments. The visitor steps into an atmosphere remote from this turbulent age.

Peace pervades the gardens of La Pietra, the Tuscan villa of author and historian Sir Harold Acton. For Sir Harold, the gardens are a symbol of Italy. Renaissance humanism finds expression in their gracious arrangement. Statues, human in scale, remind man of his place in nature. Clipped boxwood, yew and cypress are like walls of a domicile, the pauses between them like doors and corridors.

ABOVE: *Sunlight filters through the web of climbing roses that screens the pergola, with its procession of columns.*
TOP: *On a hillside stands a Roman temple of love, a belvedere where marble lovers tryst.*

RIGHT: *As in a Renaissance painting, every element in the landscape—clipped hedges, a broken pediment and marble goddesses—heightens the sense of perspective.*

ABOVE: *At its southern boundary, the garden ends in a peristyle of Corinthian columns, covered by wisteria.*

LEFT: *A highlight is the open-air theater, with statues by the 18th-century sculptor Francesco Bonazza. Clipped boxwood forms the footlights; the topiary wings are of yew.*

Adjoining the quattrocento villa are a fragrant lemon garden and a stanzone where the lemon trees are sheltered in wintertime. Boxwood and cypress hedges define areas containing a variety of vegetables, herbs and fruit trees. The scheme is like a floor plan where man moves in harmony amidst vegetation tamed by reason.

A Peaceful Landscape in Kyoto

The roji, *or stone pathway leading to a teahouse, is an important element in the design of Japanese gardens. Walking on this path, laid out with a studied casualness, is the first stage in leaving worldly concerns behind for the transcendent experience of the tea ceremony.*

IN JAPAN, CITIES DO NOT reveal their treasures immediately. Even the loveliest residential neighborhoods of Kyoto, the old capital, show the street only walls, with tantalizing glimpses of patterned roofs and graceful trees beyond. The noted painter Tetsuro Sugimoto lives in such a setting. Traditional elements of Japanese landscape design—water, trees and stone—envelop his house and its various pavilions.

Unlike the lush displays of Western gardens, those of Japan seek an understated, studied casualness. Shrubs, evergreens, ferns, moss, even sand, are preferred to colorful flower beds. Mr. Sugimoto has allowed a few flowering plants to show the changing seasons: Plum blossoms, the traditional promise of the coming of spring, emerge after the New Year; camellia and cherry blossoms arrive with the warm weather; stately iris and graceful wisteria signal summer; and the rich brocade pattern of maples heralds autumn.

Mr. Sugimoto's garden lies on a hillside, with paths and a stream following its contours. An arched stone bridge crosses the brook as it widens into a pond, and a small waterfall adds its gentle sound. Pavilions define the landscape: They are placed for decoration, devotion and particularly for the serving of tea according to the rules of the traditional tea ceremony.

The ideal of a teahouse is one of refined poverty, explained as "the art of concealing beauty, that you may discover it." It is a place to entertain, but not to display one's riches—a simple haven in which a single painting or revered object is set forth for sensitive contemplation. In Japan, teahouses are collected. Mr. Sugimoto's *Jizaian*—literally, "Come-as-you-are hut"—was once owned by a famous Yokohama silk merchant who, in the early years of this century, collected teahouses and pagodas as if they were netsuke. One post used in restoring this building is several hundred years old, and Mr. Sugimoto points out that an entire house could be built for the price of that single piece of precious antique wood.

As an artist, Mr. Sugimoto favors Buddhist religious themes for his subjects, and the art of Japanese landscaping is similarly inspired by Buddhist philosophy. The concept of a dwelling goes beyond the structure of the house, and a home is complete only when combined with a garden. In Japan, a home is not merely a functional shelter for the body—it is a nurturing source for the spirit as well.

The artist Tetsuro Sugimoto's residence in Kyoto follows the Japanese practice of combining a garden with the home. Set with pavilions and teahouses, his understated, meticulously planned garden combines the traditional elements—water, trees and stone. The view from an upper pavilion shows the cascading pattern of roof tiles; their gentle rippling and subdued hue blend naturally with the distant terrain.

ABOVE: *Beside one of the paths, on a carpet of cedar moss, a decorative rock is inscribed with the character* kotobuki, *signifying longevity.*

LEFT: *A stone bridge crosses the stream, which, after winding all the way through the garden, finally flows into the pond near the main house. The banks dividing land and water are enhanced with a great variety of carefully selected rocks and shrubs, adding to the beauty of the total composition.*

49

LEFT: *A garden of rocks and sand—made to be viewed and enjoyed from inside the house—is so small that it is called "a world in a jar." Designed with Japanese Zen reticence, this type of garden is meant to symbolize the natural world in a most abstract but eloquent way.*

BELOW: *The walkway leading from the main residence to one of the teahouses is sheltered with a roof supported by natural trunks of knotty cypress.*

OPPOSITE: *Steps lead from the stream to a pavilion that, though complicated and costly to build, is thatched to give the modest appearance of a simple hut.*

51

A Chinese Cup Garden near Millbrook

Interestingly shaped rocks, bordering stone slab steps, are part of Mr. Beck's legacy of natural stone sculptures. Sedum cuts a brightly colored trail beside the steps, while maples, ablaze for autumn, herald the dovecote.

INNISFREE IS A CUP GARDEN, sometimes called a stroll garden, its form inspired by ancient Chinese landscape art. Situated near Millbrook, New York, it encompasses a thousand acres of wooded hills surrounding a cobalt-blue lake. In the metaphor of the cup garden, the lake is the bottom of the cup while the cliffs embracing it are the vessel's steep sides. Within this majestic landscape are scores of smaller cups, all interconnected by a footpath that encircles the lake. Some are no larger than a tabletop—a weatherworn rock planted with moss, ferns and wild flowers. On a grander scale are cups in the form of rock gardens, with fern-fringed waterfalls, stepping-stones, lotus pools and Chinese zigzag bridges.

Walter Beck, creator of the garden, was a successful American painter when, at the age of sixty-five, he decided to design his stroll garden. He worked on it contentedly for twenty-two years and considered it to be his finest achievement. When the artist and his wife, Marion, first retired to Innisfree, in 1930, they intended to plant an English garden, and they modeled their residence after the manor at Wisley Garden, of the Royal Horticultural Society in England. They started their English-style plantings, but quickly abandoned them when Mr. Beck saw a scroll depicting a remarkable garden built in China by the T'ang Dynasty poet and painter Wang Wei. Mr. Beck recognized that the concept of the Chinese cup garden was better suited than the gentle English design to the rugged terrain of Innisfree. Without ever visiting China, he assimilated the principles of its ancient gardens as portrayed in Wang Wei's painting.

Walter Beck's genius especially reveals itself in the rock sculptures he created for his garden. He scoured the hillsides of Innisfree for extraordinary rocks—some like Giacometti sculptures, others reminiscent of Henry Moore's work; some as large as grand pianos and others resembling real or imaginary creatures. The boulders were dug by hand and moved by tractor, rollers, mules and winches, wrapped in quilts to protect such delicate features as a tender fern or a clump of moss.

Still dreaming of expanding his garden, Mr. Beck died in 1954, at the age of ninety-one. Marion Beck lived on at Innisfree until 1959. Today, preserved by the Innisfree Foundation, the garden remains a tribute to the inspiration of Chinese landscape design and to the bold conception of its creator.

The American painter Walter Beck devoted his life to art, yet considered his master-piece to be Innisfree, his majestic garden near Millbrook, New York. He spent twenty-two happy years creating it. Built in 1929, the imposing stone house sits on a terraced hill. The stepped bridge, defined on either end by apple trees, crosses a landscaped stream that flows into a clear lake at the bottom of the hill.

ABOVE: *Inspired by an ancient Chinese "cup garden" portrayed in a T'ang Dynasty scroll, the painter envisioned his thousand acres as an enormous cup: The fifty-acre lake forms the cup's bottom, the densely wooded encircling hills, its sides.*

RIGHT: *Stepping-stones and fragrant thyme surround a boulder whose form suggested its name: Turtle Rock.*

A triangular rock called the Owl and a formation called the Dragon join Turtle Rock in a dramatic smaller cup garden at the edge of the lake. Although the practice of using rocks as focal points in a garden derives from the Chinese, Mr. Beck expressed a distinctly personal vision in Innisfree's natural stone sculptures. To have done otherwise would have revealed "an emptiness of spirit and lack of creative powers," he believed.

Near a wooden bridge, reflections of trees darken the lake. In summer—like beacons announcing the changing of the seasons—thousands of water lilies light up the water's edge.

Inscribed upon a tall rock, three Chinese characters express an endearment meant for the painter's wife, Marion, an enthusiastic participant in developing the garden.

Wang Shi Yuan
in the Heart of Soochow

In a courtyard above the moon gate, the characters for "Cloud Grotto" have been carved on a white stone resembling a Chinese book.

IN ALL OF CHINA perhaps no city is more delightful than Soochow. West of Shanghai, in a prosperous and well-watered land, and long celebrated for its craftsmen and painters, scholars and poets, it is a place of willow-fringed canals and whitewashed houses. But above all, Soochow is renowned for its ancient gardens. A score of them still exist today, and none so well captures the grace and spirit of the city as does the *Wang Shi Yuan,* the "Garden of the Master of the Fishing Nets." Built in the twelfth century by the scholar official Shi Zhengzhi as a refuge from the burdens of administration, it acquired its present form under another owner, Qu Yuancun, in the late eighteenth century.

The Wang Shi Yuan covers 1⅓ acres, and its walls divide and redivide the space into an astonishing number of different little gardens. Some of them are open, some secret; some lead into others, some are cul-de-sacs; some are half obscured by trees or divided by walkways or garden rooms, but all are fitted into each other with the complexity of a Chinese puzzle. From the unpretentious postern gate at the north end of the garden, the delicate labyrinth gradually reveals itself, court by court. The elements of nature are introduced slowly, as if the garden maker were holding back, encouraging the slow enjoyment of simple seasonal pleasures so easily forgotten in the busy world outside.

The structure of the garden is based on the harmonious balance of yin and yang. Water is the yin element, symbolic of rivers and seas, feminine softness and yielding; rocks are the yang element, representing mountains, the bony skeleton of the earth and masculine strength. So in the Wang Shi Yuan, the silky gleam of the lake is symbolically "balanced" by waterworn rocks, fitted together to form the huge rockeries the Chinese call "miniature mountains."

Reminders of the past are important in the Wang Shi Yuan. In pre-revolutionary China, visitors to a garden would often write poems to commemorate the day; these have been engraved in fine calligraphy on smooth stone tablets and set along the covered walkways or embedded in the garden walls. The Wang Shi Yuan is not only beautiful, but has been long and deeply loved. Today, in the middle of a bustling modern city, it is still—to borrow a Chinese phrase—a place, above all, to "refresh the heart."

An example of a Chinese scholar's garden, the Wang Shi Yuan, or "Garden of the Master of the Fishing Nets," in Soochow, was first built in the 12th century and acquired its present form in the late 18th century. It comprises a main residence, smaller halls, summerhouses, and ten tiny gardens. The Pavilion of Moon Arriving and Breeze Coming is the focus of the lake at the heart of the garden.

OPPOSITE: *Leading to the Hall for Viewing the Pine and Seeing a Painting, a zigzag bridge of stone slabs provides varied vantage points for contemplating the details of the garden. The curve of the pine contrasts with the ribs of the roof behind. The surrounding rockery adds a sense of wilderness.*

ABOVE: *Capped with ivy, a pillar of cemented stones—signifying strength—shields the lake from the nearby path. The flat shelf at the water's edge provides a spot for contemplation.*

ABOVE LEFT: *A light-toned wall sets off a characteristic composition of rocks, cobbled paving and bamboo—the latter a symbol of an honorable man, who may be bowed by adversity, but never broken. The large rock rising behind the bamboos might be seen, in the imagination, as the distant peaks of a great mountain range; the mellowed wall, the misty spaces of the wilderness.*

LEFT: *Grillwork, varying in design, offers a contrast to the holes and hollows of a Taihu rock. Rocks are highly prized in China as nature's "sculpture."*

A Profusion of
Flowers in Pennsylvania

Sensitive to the nuances of feeling offered by the different flowers in his garden, Mr. Green carefully selected each, like the Country Cousin day lily, for its distinctive characteristics.

AT FIRST GLANCE it might seem a contradiction for Robert L. Green, an exponent of high fashion, to espouse the delights of gardening. But on reflection a certain logic presents itself. After all, a talent for discerning harmonies in fabrics can be extended into the reaches of the floral world, and an understanding of proportions must surely be echoed in the laying out of a garden. "Let me say that it came as a great surprise to *me,* when I bought *Tollgate Farm* in 1963," says Mr. Green. "I'd never planted a seed in my life and I had no idea that the sixty-five acres I acquired with the house would turn me into a complete garden addict."

Like many budding gardeners, he started off with packets of seed. "Then, when I began to realize that the results were somewhat random—to say the least—I began to do what I always do when a subject fascinates me: I bought books, and I read about it. I soon found, however, that books give a good deal of sound advice, but are rather repetitious. I was ready for the next step, which turned out to be nurseries."

Before long, Mr. Green planted a spread of perennials, then a formal rose garden and, finally, massed displays of daffodils, irises and day lilies. "I definitely do not belong to the group that thinks a garden should be a kind of floral military school," he affirms. "I don't like flowers that stand to attention. Flowers should look as though they were on a marvelous outing—instead of engaging in some rather hostile activity."

He does, however, have decided views on the appropriate floral mix. "Certain flowers are gracious and polite," he says. "Others have bad manners, and several are distinctly nouveau riche. Then there are the shy ones, dear little things, like baby's breath, who need gentle companions. Really, the principles are the same as those you would apply to a decent party. Planning a garden is very much a matter of bringing the right personalities together in harmony."

Over the twenty years Mr. Green has owned Tollgate Farm, his love of gardening has blossomed like the flowers in his fields. "Flowers become one's children," he says. "They are a responsibility and a joy. And eventually, when you start seeing the progeny of your own blooms in other people's gardens, you realize that you are a grandparent! Finally—and perhaps this is the most satisfying—you do develop a reputation as a garden person."

*To his own surprise, noted arbiter of fashion and taste Robert L. Green became an
enthusiastic gardener after he acquired Tollgate Farm in Bucks County, Pennsylvania. A field of daffodils, arranged at nature's caprice, illustrates his belief that
"flowers should look as though they were on a marvelous outing."*

ABOVE: *The swimming pond—one of the many bounties of the sixty-five-acre property—reflects a view of the main house, framed by willow trees. Lilies brighten the water's edge.*

RIGHT: *Applying the same principles to planning a garden as to hosting a party, Mr. Green chooses flowers for their personalities and enjoys placing them in harmonious combinations. Some of his favorites include (top to bottom): one of a wide variety of roses, Gloriosa daisy, Imperial Gold hybrid lily and purple cone flower.*

TOP: *The rose garden is planted around a symmetrical arrangement of Japanese maples and star magnolias.* ABOVE LEFT: *Some of the lilies and daffodils growing in profusion at Tollgate Farm grace a slope leading to the pond.* ABOVE RIGHT: *Brilliant masses of daffodils proclaim the arrival of spring.*

FOLLOWING PAGES: *As a special present to himself, Mr. Green lavished the garden with 10,000 daffodil bulbs, like those lighting up the entrance to the meadow.*

67

ABOVE: *A sea of daffodils prefaces a view of the barn.*

ABOVE RIGHT: *Stone steps, surrounded by grape hyacinths and miniature daffodils, lead from the meadow to the corral.*

RIGHT: *The meadow just below the main house is the domain of Tollgate's horses, Tom, Toppett and Chaos.*

OPPOSITE: *The Tollgate hybrid daffodil reflects the expanded scope of Mr. Green's horticultural activities, since he first began, simply, with packets of seed.*

Rungstedlund
on the Coast of Denmark

At the entrance to the estate, a haw-thorn arch frames a view of the harbor.

IT WAS AT RUNGSTEDLUND, her family home on the coast of Denmark, that the baroness Karen Blixen, adopting the nom de plume Isak Dinesen, wrote the two books that established her literary reputation—*Seven Gothic Tales* and *Out of Africa*. But for the quiet of country life she would never have become a writer, claimed the diminutive aristocrat, who devoted thirty years to carefully landscaping the gardens and creating a sanctuary for migratory birds at her beloved estate.

Before her parents married, the baroness's father acquired Rungstedlund, a quaint, many-chimneyed farmhouse that, 300 years before, had been an inn where coaches en route from Copenhagen to Elsinore changed horses. But country life and Victorian manners were not sufficiently exciting for the high-spirited Karen. "I really don't know how we managed to pass the time . . . to wait with my two sisters, poised like so many flowers, until plucked by some husband," she wrote in her autobiography. Instead, she rebelliously chose her own husband, the dashing baron Bror Blixen-Finecke, and in 1914 the adventurous couple moved to Kenya, where they established the Karen Coffee Estate, a 6000-acre coffee plantation.

Seventeen years later, she returned to Rungstedlund and, with typical zeal, embarked simultaneously upon a literary career and the planning of her *jardin sylvestre*. The baroness indulged her passion for flowers by planting the Rungstedlund with wild flowers, using native varieties to assure the succession of bloom that persists to this day. Anxious lest the encroachment of Copenhagen's suburbs deprive the thousands of migratory birds that fly across Denmark each year of needed resting spots, she replanted fifty acres with trees and shrubs that would attract the passing flocks. She also allowed the nettles closest to the house to grow unhindered, "for birds favor wilderness, and the nightingale is said to nest in a jungle of nettles," she wrote. Soon, nightingales were drawn by her tender inducements.

One of Isak Dinesen's last gestures before her death, in 1962, was to plant "The Listeners' Oak" in her garden, as a legacy to her loyal readers. Taken from a scion of a famous thousand-year-old tree, it is a potent symbol of endurance. "It is to me a pleasant thought," she wrote, "that the long-gone past and the distant future of Denmark might be thus united at Rungstedlund."

Denmark's legendary Baroness Karen Blixen lavished thirty years on the creation of the gardens and bird sanctuary at her family estate, Rungstedlund. Here, too, she conceived her major literary works, Seven Gothic Tales *and* Out of Africa, *using the nom de plume Isak Dinesen. The centuries-old farmhouse was once an inn where coaches en route from Copenhagen to Elsinore stopped to change horses. Wild roses are part of the burgeoning rose garden the baroness asked landscape architect Georg Boye to design for the delight of boaters on the nearby sound.*

ABOVE: *A small wooden bridge spans the water. The tall trees, including weeping ash, alder and maple, were planted throughout fifty acres of the garden to provide a refuge for the multitudinous birds that flock to the estate, a sanctuary amid Copenhagen's encroaching suburbs.*

LEFT: *Especially favored by ducks, the pond—which the writer enlarged to demarcate lawn areas near the residence from the woodlands beyond—features a tiny house that offers the birds a cozy shelter.*

On a bucolic sweep of lawn between the pond and the residence, a stand of majestic chestnut trees perpetuates a sense of Rungstedlund's long history.

ABOVE: *A shady woodland path skirts Poet's Hill, named by the baroness's father in honor of Johannes Ewald, Denmark's premier lyric poet, who on this spot composed* The Beatitudes of Rungsted. *Isak Dinesen also paid homage to the poet, calling her study "Ewald's Room."*

RIGHT: *A clump of butterbur announces the rustic bridge leading to the farmhouse, while reed mace encircles the pond.*

A Winter Garden
in Bucks County

Intrepid snowdrops can be seen at the first hint of warming weather, in February or early March. They continue blooming uninterrupted while the sunshine melts the snow.

I N NORTHERN GARDENS, winter is a quiet season. Flowers have ceased their colorful rioting and the trees have shed their leaves. There is softness to the hues—the brown of earth, the grays and pinks of sky, the whiteness of snow. Derek Fell's two-acre garden in Bucks County, Pennsylvania, is at its most lovely in winter, as it straddles fast-coursing Pidcock Creek. The stream gushes from a nearby spring, on the side of Buckingham Mountain, and makes its way to the Delaware River. On one side of the stream sits the house, contemporary in design and seemingly thrust into the side of a mountain. It overlooks a secluded pond. Ranging from the other bank is a wild area that offers a striking contrast to the formal landscape features surrounding the house itself.

Winter is Mr. Fell's favorite season. At the first snowfall he eagerly dons cross-country skis and takes to the labyrinthine trails, observing the land with the keen eye of a plant photographer and garden writer. "When I first began the garden," he says, "there was a great temptation to add color through all the seasons. Instead, I decided to spend a year just watching things grow. After a while, I realized that the natural environment needed little embellishment during spring, summer and fall. I thought my energies would be best spent in creating a winter garden."

To enhance his winter garden, Mr. Fell planted hundreds of bulbs that bloom in the snow: snow crocuses and winter aconites, snowdrops and two of his favorites, the Christmas rose and its purple cousin, the Lenten rose. When the earth is thickly blanketed in white, Mr. Fell finds much to observe in the fields and woods: a flock of chirping chickadees; deer standing statuelike on the horizon; brilliant red cardinals shining like Christmas lights against snow-covered brambles.

"They say the Eskimos have twenty-five different words for snow. There are early snows that simply tint the landscape; heavy snows that seem to suffocate the whole world in silence; icy snows that cling to the weeping willow branches and make them sparkle like a million tiny flashing lights. There are friendly snows that recall Christmas scenes, and the savage blizzards that always seem to slam in from the south and keep you locked indoors for days on end." Derek Fell makes these comparisons with equanimity, ensconced as he is in his own peaceable kingdom.

In wintertime, when most northern gardens slumber, Derek Fell's fastness in Bucks County, Pennsylvania, revels in snow-clad beauty. A wooden bridge spans Pidcock Creek, whose course divides the two-acre garden's landscaped area from its woods. Berry-bearing shrubs, planted along the stream banks, attract red cardinals and other songbirds all year long.

ABOVE LEFT: *A woodland coppice reveals the graphic contrast of walnut saplings and shrubs brushed with snow. Mr. Fell enhanced the natural pattern by clearing underbrush from the bases of the trees.* ABOVE: *Nature generously bedecks a spruce tree with cones like Christmas ornaments.*

LEFT: *Small clusters of color, hardy winter aconites shrug off their seasonal blanket of snow.*

Mantled in snow, evergreen branches make an inviting shelter for the many flocks of doves, finches and pheasants that find a winter haven in the garden.

Silent vistas abound as Pidcock Creek traces a course through neighboring woods and meadows on its way to meet the nearby Delaware River. Deer and other forest denizens are frequent visitors.

A quiet sky silhouettes the tracery of tulip poplar and wild cherry branches in the landscape surrounding the winter garden. Footprints chart man's peaceful solitude.

The Dramatic
Ashland Hollow in Delaware

Even the calico cat, Flicker, finds refreshment in the cool spring water of one of the property's five ponds.

COMING UPON A secluded valley among the rolling hills of upper Delaware, landscape architect William H. Frederick, Jr. and his wife, Nancy, knew instantly that they had found the site for their future home and gardens, *Ashland Hollow*. The spot they chose afforded a view upstream of the flowing water and steep wooded banks, and downstream a contrasting vista of open, sunny meadowland.

And though much of the landscape design is his own conception, Mr. Frederick is quick to acknowledge the contribution of Conrad Hamerman, a landscape architect and a student of the Brazilian master Roberto Burle Marx. "It was Mr. Hamerman who first laid out the ponds, blending them with the natural contours of the land," says Mr. Frederick, referring to the ponds and a series of sparkling waterfalls achieved by damming the stream at frequent intervals and on different levels. It was also Mr. Hamerman who envisioned the masses of azaleas that cover the hillsides like broad swaths of paint daubed on a canvas. Yet in the spring, the most glorious sight of all is the fragrant purple wisteria. The vines are trained into tree forms and planted high on the slope bordering a footpath appropriately called Wisteria Walk.

Native wild flowers add their diminutive beauty to the gardens. Delicate blue-blossoming quaker-ladies crowd the cracks between stone paving; in the meadow area violets, jack-in-the-pulpits and spring beauties bloom and seed themselves. Later in the season, black-eyed susans, Queen Anne's lace and day lilies accent the meadow with color. But perhaps the most spectacular wild flower planting is the majestic stand of cardinal flowers, their scarlet spikes like bright beacons in the shade.

Not surprisingly, the gardens play a large part in the daily life of the Fredericks. While his wife tends the vegetable garden, the landscape architect spends most of his day in his studio, adjacent to the house. In warm weather, both enjoy dining in the studio garden, its walls covered with vines and espaliers. Often during the course of a summer day they will meet for a dip in the swimming pool, which is designed to simulate a millpond. Although Ashland Hollow is more than twenty years old, the owners regard it still as a garden in the making. While lavishing love and care on what they have already accomplished, they view it as only a prelude to the beauty they hope to create in the future.

A meandering stream linked by ponds and waterfalls, hillsides planted with vibrant swaths of azaleas, and a luxuriance of wild flowers are among the delights of the seventeen-acre garden of Mr. and Mrs. William H. Frederick, Jr. in upper Delaware. From its source at the springhouse, the stream cascades downhill, spilling over broad stone slabs into a sequence of terraced ponds.

ABOVE: *Great boulders add a primeval aspect to the setting. Enhancing the scene are ripples of sunlight and shade and the exuberant natural symphony produced by splashing water, songbirds and a coterie of resident frogs.*

RIGHT: *A blaze of azaleas and wisteria vines trained into tree forms lend the sparkle of an Impressionist painting to Mr. Frederick's adroit landscaping of Ashland Hollow.*

ABOVE: *After flowing through the shaded ponds, the stream passes underneath the house as through a tunnel. Emerging on the other side, it greets a meadow bathed in sunlight.*

RIGHT: *Viewed from the strategically situated Living Room, a sculptured earthen island covered in moss rises like a small pyramid from the dark waters of the lowest pond. Azaleas brighten the surrounding slopes, and tulip poplars, towering overhead, create a welcome umbrella of shade.*

A Wildflower Garden
in Pennsylvania

A phalanx of lily-flowered tulips and blue phlox brightens the approach to a fenced-in section with a garden shed.

DAVID BENNER, A PROFESSOR of horticulture, appreciates and enjoys gardens, as might easily be expected. He does not, however, appreciate and enjoy the many chores that would ordinarily accompany cultivating a garden at his home in Bucks County, Pennsylvania. Fortunately, Mr. Benner has found an ideal medium— a garden of wild flowers that, being wild, look after themselves. They surround his house near the town of New Hope and cover a hillside on the property. It is a garden favored by many botanical species, some of them rare; by birds, which delight in the birdbath and small waterfall; and most of all by the Benner family, who spend many hours in its mossy glades and intimate spaces.

When the Benners moved to their present home, twenty-five years ago, there was an expansive lawn, beautiful but demanding. By changing the chemical composition of the soil, Mr. Benner encouraged native mosses to replace the grass. Tall trees provide the essential shade and require only occasional pruning. His next step was to establish beds of evergreen ground covers, many of them with variegated foliage, to avoid an overabundance of green.

The last step was the sowing of the wild flowers themselves. Four subdued colors were chosen to predominate: soft blue, white, pale yellow and pink. The most spectacular hues appear in springtime, in native American species: white bloodroot, yellow celandine poppies, pink bleeding hearts and blue phlox. Flowering shrubs such as azaleas and rhododendrons produce even more dramatic splashes of color. Tulip poplars, beech, oak and black birch trees add their native majesty to the setting.

The Benners' garden surrounds their wood frame house and climbs the ridge in tiers. A dwarf-evergreen garden is fenced in at the side of the house. Up the hillside, another glade nurtures thousands of blue quaker-ladies that have naturalized in the moss lawn. Higher still, the wild food garden abounds with wild berries. Each section of the garden has its own personality, and is connected to the others by steps, trails and stone paths.

With thoughtful planning, and certainly no compromise in beauty, David Benner has created a self-perpetuating wild flower enclave. His only "gardening" is the task of raking up leaves in fall. Truly, these wild flowers have made a natural garden in every way.

At his Bucks County home, botanist David Benner has created a wild flower garden designed to take care of itself. In a view from a knoll, native dogwoods light up the overhead canopy of young leaves. A path wanders through wild flowers and shrubs, carefully planted to simulate nature's random perfection.

ABOVE: *A moss lawn is bordered by evergreen ground covers that remain decorative throughout the year.*

RIGHT: *Quaker ladies bloomed in the moss lawn unexpectedly one spring, creating a fresh carpet for a birdbath. Native birds, however, prefer to gather at the waterfall nearby.*

OPPOSITE: *Parts of the property are left to their natural state, contributing to the garden's varied character. In a wooded setting, a rare species of foam flower exhibits the frothy lightness from which it takes its name.*

ABOVE: *Wild columbines, their petals forming tiny lanterns, stand brightly colored amidst the subdued shades of the garden.* RIGHT: *Soft, thick moss flourishes at the base of a beech tree. Mr. Benner fostered the growth of native mosses by altering the chemical composition of the soil.*

A du Pont Creation at Nemours

A hedge of Hino azaleas blooms about a marble bust of Talleyrand, Napoleon's foreign minister and a friend of a du Pont forebear.

IT IS A SECRET GARDEN of the grandest order, built by a man of passion and rebelliousness. A forbidding stone wall, its top embedded with broken glass, encloses magnificent lawns and allées, thickets of azaleas, woods and wandering streams. Alfred I. du Pont conceived *Nemours* to ensure privacy for himself and his great love, Alicia Bradford du Pont, his cousin and second wife. Their romance had been an odyssey of intrigue. Each was married to another when they fell in love, in the first years of this century. She was considered just a bit too vivacious. He was the orphaned son grown finally successful through business adventures. The clandestine marriage to Alicia, in 1906, created unwanted publicity and a familial rift. When Alfred and Alicia developed their 300-acre estate in Wilmington, Delaware, other members of the du Pont family were uninvited.

The grounds and the seventy-seven-room mansion, modeled after a Louis XVI château, are effectively French Renaissance, with parterres, fountains and Baroque sculptures. These formal French gardens slope away from the main residence for a third of a mile, and are surrounded by unstructured landscape reminiscent of English country gardens. The mastery of Nemours is in this marriage of geometry and free-flowing naturalism.

Alfred I. du Pont was exceptional in his personal supervision of the building and landscaping of Nemours, handing over his own designs for architects merely to polish. When a construction problem arose, he took delight in tackling the job himself. Typical of his approach was his solution for the lack of natural running water at the estate. He devised a dam for a tributary of the nearby Brandywine River, creating a reservoir. This supplied a subterranean aqueduct sufficient to provide for all of the Nemours fountains and the eight lakes as well.

Alfred and Alicia du Pont enjoyed Nemours for some ten years, until her death in 1918. Alfred died in 1935, and his third wife, Jessie Ball du Pont, lived at the estate the rest of her life. In 1970 a Nemours Foundation was established, which now maintains the mansion and gardens. Alfred I. du Pont created a work of art and of love, but he had no desire to show it off; the stout stone wall concealed Nemours from the world. It was the secret place of a du Pont who, by character and circumstance, was set far apart from the rest.

Hundreds of acres of untamed woodland surround the Versailles-inspired formal gardens and main residence of Nemours, the Delaware estate of the late Alfred I. du Pont. Broad terraced steps of bluestone descend from the columned portico of the châteaulike residence built in 1910, through an allée of hybrid horse chestnut trees. Flower-filled sculptured urns impart a classical air to the imposing vista.

Visible through the blossom-laden branches of a tamarisk tree is the garden's graceful Grecian-style Temple of Love, housing a life-size bronze statue of the goddess Diana. Like the dessert at the end of a lengthy banquet, this marble pavilion marks the conclusion of the long vista that originates at the allée of horse chestnut trees.

ABOVE: *The natural configurations of the several lakes at Nemours provide a rustic contrast to the stately gardens in the French style.* RIGHT: *Where the immense lawn of the formal garden ends, the natural wooded landscape begins, with a small stream meandering peacefully among tall trees. In contrast to the formal gardens, casual plantings of narcissus and brilliant azaleas endow this area with the freedom of form usually associated with English country gardens.*

A humpbacked bridge crosses the man-made watercourse fed by a tributary of the nearby Brandywine River. Large stones line the stream bed and, scattered among colorful tulips and wild flowers, transform its banks into a rock garden.

Grapevines, trained on arched steel rods, create the 250-foot-long arbor that borders the Nemours orchard. In springtime, six varieties of the fruit cover the arbor with dense foliage, and in autumn produce a grape-scented tunnel cloaked in gold.

Kiluna Farm of Long Island

A stone eagle surveys the more formal area of lawn and clipped shrubbery between the house and the dell.

KILUNA FARM, THE ESTATE of Mr. William S. Paley and the late Mrs. Paley, is an enclave in one of the few oases of unspoiled Long Island landscape still existing within a half hour's drive from New York City. Well sited at the head of a sweep of rolling grassland, the residence commands a rare view of Long Island Sound and the hills of Connecticut beyond. Behind the house, the gardens are shielded by acres of native woodland: oak, dogwood and tulip poplar, with here and there a splendid gray-boled beech.

Nearly thirty-three years ago, Mrs. Paley, a keen, practical horticulturist, felt dissatisfied with her garden layout. It seemed to have neither mystery nor logic. She decided to cut into the woods and seek a focal point, and it was in the dell that she found it—her "secret garden." Conversations with three friends—Russell Page, the English garden designer; the late Henry Francis du Pont, owner of *Winterthur;* and the late Thomas Church, the American landscape architect—led to the eventual design solution. The dell was transformed into a well-defined, planted punch bowl, with a large oval pond in the center, set in an inner frame of lawn, with an outer frame of ground covers, low evergreens, flowering trees and shrubs. Mr. du Pont and Mr. Church contributed valuable advice. But it was Russell Page who was most instrumental in bringing the secret garden to life.

Clearing the dell and leveling the approach to it proved to be major operations. With the help of a winch mounted on a jeep, trees and underbrush were uprooted. The outlines of the oval pond and lawn and the surrounding paths and planting areas were laid out. Transplanted Japanese azaleas covered the sides of the punch bowl, and a whole field of Knap Hill azaleas was purchased to supplement them. Truckloads of rhododendrons and mountain laurel arrived from South Carolina. Massed ground covers and stands of pine and juniper filled empty spaces beneath trees and shrubs and softened the transition between planted area and lawn.

The passage of time has matured and naturalized Mrs. Paley's secret dell. Yet, ever the inveterate improver, she continued to work tirelessly. As a true gardener, she knew that the breed is one whose territorial ambitions, like its challenges, are endless; and that the joy of a gardener's life consists in the knowledge that perfection remains just around the corner, and that work must never cease.

Profuse plantings cover the upper slopes of the dell at Mr. and Mrs. William S. Paley's Kiluna Farm, on Long Island. According to English garden designer Russell Page, who helped create this horticultural tour de force, the collaboration resulted in "Barbara Paley's own, individual, character-revealing garden."

ABOVE: *Concentric ovals formed by a pond, grass, plants and the surrounding woodland are visible from atop the steps leading down to the serendipitous garden.*

RIGHT: *Lilies of the valley blossom in a fragrant cluster beneath a dogwood tree.*

ABOVE: *Ajuga, one of the many ground covers that flourish at Kiluna Farm, harmonizes with a luxuriant drift of colorful azaleas.*

RIGHT: *The stone-edged grass steps leading up from the dell toward the house pass dwarf hemlocks and a variegated ground cover of plantain lily.*

A view from the far end of the dell catches a secret garden of azaleas and dogwood vividly reflected in the still pond. The dogwood demarcates the woodland from the lawn approaching the sylvan glen.

Eleutherian Mills
on the Brandywine River

Tall trees and flowering shrubs add beauty to an area of the garden accented by an old saltpeter cauldron once used in the making of gunpowder.

A FEW MILES NORTH of Wilmington, Delaware, the Brandywine River leaves the rich open farmlands of southeastern Pennsylvania. Snaking its way between steeply wooded hills, it quickens its pace over boulders and rapids in a final rush to the sea. Early in the nineteenth century, Eleuthère Irénée du Pont de Nemours, newly arrived from France, saw more than beauty as he walked along the riverbanks. He had in mind the manufacture of gunpowder and he envisioned the trees as a source of charcoal, the water as energy, and the steep banks as buffers to blunt the force of any explosions.

The new home he built for his family, on a hill directly overlooking the powder mills, closely resembled the country house they had left in France. For the garden, too, Mr. du Pont wanted plants familiar to him in his native land and immediately sent for supplies of seeds, grafts and cuttings. The two-acre garden he planted near the main house at *Eleutherian Mills* was totally French in character, and the plantings today preserve the original design. The garden is composed of quadrants, each bordered by dwarf fruit trees espaliered as low hedges. A latticework gazebo provides a peaceful spot for contemplation, and an arbor of apple trees forms a tunnel along one of the pathways. Vegetables and berries are planted in ornamental rows and flowering perennials provide splashes of color.

Direct descendants of Irénée du Pont occupied the main house until it was damaged by a severe powder explosion in 1890. In 1921, when powder-making along the Brandywine ceased, the Du Pont company offered the land to members of the family, and Henry Algernon du Pont, a grandson of the founder, acquired the mansion for his daughter, Louise Evelina du Pont Crowninshield. While Mrs. Crowninshield concentrated on restoring the interior of the house, her husband, Francis, established a garden folly on the slopes below the residence, converting the damaged powder mills into classical ruins complete with courtyards, classical statues, Corinthian columns, Roman baths and secret passages.

Mrs. Crowninshield was the last du Pont to occupy the home, living there until 1952, when the care of the property became the responsibility of the Eleutherian Mills-Hagley Foundation. But Irénée du Pont's passion for plants and gardening flourishes among his descendants, and today, true to family tradition, many of them maintain beautiful homes and gardens in the area.

Emigrating from France at the beginning of the 19th century, Eleuthère Irénée du Pont de Nemours settled in Delaware; there he created for his family a home and garden reminiscent of their native land.

Irénée du Pont chose to situate his home and garden on the banks of the Brandywine not only for the beauty of the setting, but also because the river supplied water-power, by means of millraces, to his powder mills.

LEFT: *The branches of stalwart beech trees sweep to the ground, forming a tent of leaves.* BELOW: *The blossoming boughs of a dogwood tree overhang the dark waters of one of the millraces.*

ABOVE: *Blossoms of dogwood trees intermingle above a meadow festive with daffodils.*

RIGHT: *Azaleas emblazon a terraced garden below the house at Eleutherian Mills; redbuds and dogwoods interject softer hues.*

114

After the powder mills at Eleutherian Mills were closed, a corner of the property was transformed into a garden folly evoking a Roman ruin. Here candytuft and native ferns flourish, and a magnolia blooms beyond a balustrade.

The Woodlands at Bodnant

Highlight of the Canal Terrace, named for its narrow stretch of water, is the picturesque Pin Mill, originally built as a garden house in Gloucestershire about 1730.

I T IS POSSIBLE to drive past *Bodnant* without noticing it, so naturally does it clothe a Welsh hillside with tall trees. The distant view is of sliding, crossing hills and the sandy estuary of the river Conwy looped like a flung ribbon below them. Nearer, gables and turrets of a large house peek out from above leafy masses. To drive on without pausing would be to miss one of the most glorious sights in all of Britain.

Bodnant was the conception of Henry Pochin, who, in the 1870s, first planted the conifers that now soar to over 100 feet. Pochin's daughter, herself a great gardener, married the first Lord Aberconway, and three generations of this family transformed the hillside into a cornucopia of delight. The present lord and his American wife, Ann, live surrounded by the garden, which he tends with a mixture of delicacy and control. Nor must be forgotten the Puddles, father and son, successive head gardeners from 1920 until the present day, who were both awarded the highest honor of the Royal Horticultural Society.

It is Puddle I and Aberconway II to whom most of the credit for the garden is due. Harry Aberconway possessed a stupendous knowledge of everything that grows. He was also a garden designer of genius. When his mother inherited Bodnant, a lawn sloped steeply down from the house. He cut into this slope as though it were cake, forming five large terraces, called variously the Rose, the Croquet, the Lily, the Lower Rose and the Canal Terrace—each a tray of flowers or shorn grass held out at waist level. The grandest is the lowest, where a long "canal" ends with a "theater" formed by yew hedges, and at the other with an eighteenth-century pavilion known as the Pin Mill. The descent from the Pin Mill leads into a controlled wilderness held by the banks of a deep valley called the Dell. Between the mastlike trunks of Pochin's pinetum runs the Hiraethlyn, a tributary of the Conwy.

Rhododendrons and azaleas, camellias and magnolias burst forth along the banks. This is springtime at Bodnant. Later, darker greens and brilliant reds lend a different character. In October, the patient trees wear their lovely widow's coloring—maples turn orange and deep red, and carpet the grass with fallen leaves. The evergreens provide a dark back cloth to this dazzling color and remain masters of the Dell till the rhododendrons return.

Broad terraces, dense woodland and water everywhere make the garden at Bodnant, in North Wales, a majestic display throughout the seasons. A National Trust property since 1949, Bodnant remains in the care of the third Lord Aberconway, who presides over the garden his forebears developed. In the Dell, a waterfall enlivens the course of the tiny river Hiraethlyn.

ABOVE: *A little river, rushing by, reflects nature's impermanence in its ever-changing surface.* RIGHT: *A French sphinx lends her enigmatic presence to the Rose Terrace, one of five descending, like great steps, from the residence.* FAR RIGHT: *Ferns flourish in the moist atmosphere of the garden.*

ABOVE: *Within the controlled woodland wilderness, tall pines make a stately background for vivid floral hues. Believing that a garden should be planted extensively with flora well suited to its soil and climate, the second Lord Aberconway gave pride of place to rhododendrons, azaleas, magnolias and camellias.*

LEFT: *Each of the terraces below the vine-clad house has a distinctive feature. Midway in the sequence, below the Rose and Croquet terraces, is the Lily Terrace, with its formal pond where hybrid water lilies blossom.*

ABOVE: *The succession of terraces cut civilized swaths into a hillside below the residence. From the highest terrace, the river Conwy appears in the distance, partially hidden by trees cloaked in autumn's colors.*

OPPOSITE: *Each season is a magician showing Bodnant in a different guise. In autumn, bulbs planted for spring flowering in the Chapel Park hide their promise beneath a carpet of maple leaves.*

At Willow Oaks in Virginia

Equestrian sports figure prominently in the Middleburg area. "It was the setting that really won us," says Mrs. Harriman, "and the fact that you can ride in any direction for as long and as far as you wish."

TALL TREES RISE TOGETHER, the white bark of sycamore companioning the dark trunks of pine, maple and oak. Goose Creek, a lean river meandering along its course, slices through the woods. It forms a natural boundary to the farmland, framed in the far distance by the foothills of the Blue Ridge Mountains. To W. Averell Harriman, elder statesman and a former governor of New York, this landscape seen from the balustraded terrace of his home in Middleburg, Virginia, is "the most wonderful view anywhere." For his wife, Pamela, it is a familiar landscape that, she says, "reminds me enormously of the southwest of England—Dorset—where I was brought up." Situated on fifty acres in the heart of Virginia horse country, the Harriman's home, *Willow Oaks,* offers a peaceful change from their active lives in Washington, D.C.

"When my husband and I came here six years ago," Mrs. Harriman recalls, "the garden was quite overgrown and seemed closed in." They removed some of the trees to extend the vistas of the existing garden, and established a pond and stream, which already appear as much a part of the landscape as does the river below. A natural rock formation atop a ridge sweeping down toward Goose Creek lends itself to a rock garden. In the spring, heather and myrtle, primrose and narcissus flower. In autumn the palette changes to the vibrant orange and red of chrysanthemums and maple, the pale yellow of the home's namesake, willow oaks.

"The garden really got under way after Bill Hoogeveen arrived," Mrs. Harriman says of their resident landscape gardener. "He and his four helpers kept clearing, uncovering rivulets, finding areas we hadn't known existed." She credits him with a small recently restored garden between the house and the swimming pool. Here, in spring, multicolored tulips fill the several beds around a pool in which water lilies float. Nearby, close to the kitchen, is an herb garden planted in neatly trimmed wedges. On a higher level of land is a velvety croquet lawn; on a lower plane, a jumping ring for the horses. Amid the parkland, small, graceful bridges span tiny creeks, and clusters of flowers appear in random plantings throughout the lawn. For Governor and Mrs. Harriman, their garden is a continual delight. It is for them both "a place where you can walk happily at any time of the year."

Captivated by the landscape of Middleburg, Virginia, Governor and Mrs. W. Averell Harriman created their fifty-acre garden at Willow Oaks. A view from the back of the residence encompasses woodland, a neighboring farm and the foothills of the Blue Ridge Mountains.

A blaze of dogwood sparks the bank of Goose Creek, which winds through the tranquil woodland. Gentle ripples transform the reflected image into an Impressionistic tableau.

ABOVE LEFT: *A log cabin nestles among forsythia, oak trees, honeysuckle, mosses and lilies of the valley.*

ABOVE: *Pyracantha berries offer a vivid contrast to the fieldstone residence.*

LEFT: *Patterns of sunlight flickering through the branches of oak trees lend a softening touch to sweeping lawns.*

127

Visible from the terrace of the residence is Governor Harriman's favorite view. A rock garden is ensconced below among oak, pine and sugar maple trees.

ABOVE: *Maple and walnut trees add autumn color to a lawn near the house.* RIGHT: *Retired jumpers Impetuous and Master Chatfield enjoy the holly-sheltered jumping ring, which will eventually become a wild flower garden.* FAR RIGHT: *A path for hiking and riding traverses a wooded area where honeysuckle, ferns and mosses flourish among saplings.*

Hilo Estate
on the Island of Hawaii

The beach house, built in 1910, was remodeled in 1937. In the foreground, a Kamani-haole tree shades lauae ferns.

THE POET James Russell Lowell's oft-quoted query, "And what is so rare as a day in June?" has stumped many an otherwise bright student of English literature in Hilo schools. The reason is that it is quite difficult to distinguish a June day on the island of Hawaii from any day in January or November or March. Nearly all of them are perfect—especially around Hilo, lying at the base of Mauna Loa, the great active volcano.

Just outside Hilo, four miles through sugarcane and papaya fields toward the sea, lies the Shipman estate. A red volcanic cinder road leads to it through arched Macaranga and pandanus trees, giant tree ferns and banyans. It is not unusual to see a mongoose skitter across the road into the big-leafed tropical plants, or to spy the wary shadow of a wild dog, wildcat or wild pig. This is untamed country and, though totally natural, it almost appears to be a set for a Hollywood movie, replete with hanging vines ready for Lord Greystoke.

Along the approach to the sea and the house, there are kukui nut trees, coco palms, breadfruit and banana trees, both torch and flaming kahili ginger, and towering piles of coconuts. The Victorian plantation house snuggles at the edge of a storybook sandy cove that brings to mind fantasies of Melville, Maugham, Stevenson and Gauguin. The residence was built in 1910, on land that has been in the Shipman family for nearly a hundred years. At one point the estate consisted of nearly 70,000 acres, spreading all the way from the ocean and continuing up the mountain.

Herbert Shipman, who died in 1976, was alive when Hawaii was still a monarchy, the island's last queen, Liliuokalani, being in the final months of her reign when he was born. A businessman, cattle rancher and conservationist, Mr. Shipman was perhaps most proud of his vigorous fight to save the *nene,* the state bird of Hawaii, from extinction. For his efforts he was given a life membership in the Wildfowl Trust of England. He was also a distinguished horticulturist, and in 1957 received the gold medal of the American Orchid Society. In greenhouses behind the main residence are dozens of rare flowers and plants with which he experimented. Today, Herbert Shipman's nephew, Roy S. Blackshear, maintains the estate in all its pristine charm, a reminder of the unhurried grace and beauty that once abounded in the Hawaiian islands.

ABOVE: *At the Shipman estate, near Hilo on the island of Hawaii, a freshwater lagoon, protected by a stone wall, borders part of the extensive dynastic property at Keaau Beach. The main residence, an Edwardian plantation house, overlooks a sandy cove of the lagoon.*

ABOVE: *Petals of a proud hibiscus glory in the moist environment.*

OPPOSITE: *Hibiscus blooms, floating on rainwater, typify the natural beauty of the estate.*

BELOW: *A vivid amaryllis fulfills its promise in this lush tropical paradise.*

Macarthur palms and vivid red ginger thrive near the entrance to Mr. Shipman's home. Since his death, members of the family have maintained the estate—a symbol of old-fashioned privilege as it once existed in the islands.

The stillness of the idyllic and intensely private island landscape is altered only by the sound of waves breaking against the ropy lava called Pahoehoe, deposited along the Puna Coast; not far away rises the great volcano Mauna Loa.

The Hidden Valley above Rio

The house, totally encircled by mountains, commands a prospect of the entire valley, where nothing intrudes on nature.

THE HIDDEN GARDEN of Senhora Odette Young Monteiro lies high in the mountains above Rio de Janeiro, surrounded by granite cliffs and entirely occupying its own immense valley. Imperfection cannot intrude. The Monteiro garden is in a perfect world of its own. Designed by Roberto Burle Marx, the noted Brazilian landscape architect who conceived the well-known serpentine beachfront at Copacabana, it offers a unique, isolated glimpse of his work.

From the residence, a wide path leads invitingly through the entire garden and into the forest far beyond. As it winds past dramatic groupings of exotic tropical plants, the path accents the rolling lines of green hillsides and hugs the curved banks of a large pond reflecting the shifting colors of mountains and sky. It gives the valley depth and perspective with the same artifice a gifted artist uses to give life to a broad landscape painting.

This artistic presence in the Monteiro garden is no accident, for Roberto Burle Marx is a recognized master in many mediums. His oils hang in Rio de Janeiro's National Museum of Fine Arts. He designs jewelry, as well as stage settings for the ballet and for carnival balls. He is an accomplished musician, sculptor, painter, designer and botanist. Bringing all these disciplines to his profession of landscape architect, he makes the earth itself his canvas.

"Because I am a painter, people sometimes think I paint with plants," says the multi-talented Senhor Burle Marx. "I do not try to do that. But my work with gardens is always linked to my experience as painter. That is, I always work from the artistic point of view. Debussy, in his music, knew how to create an emotion with constructions. I like to construct a garden in the same way. When I create a garden, I am composing. And I like to give clarity to the whole composition, the whole landscape."

Senhor Burle Marx says he strives for several achievements in every garden, "and the laws are the same, whether the garden is large or small. To begin with, a garden, for me, must be a work of art. Second, a garden must have different dimensions and volumes. Third, it must have clarity, if it is to be understood—and I feel it must be understood to be enjoyed." The Monteiro garden, in its isolated purity, does indeed encompass the design principles of Senhor Burle Marx, with grace and with subtlety.

In the mountains above Rio de Janeiro, granite cliffs ring the hidden valley that the eminent landscape architect Roberto Burle Marx has made into a garden for Odette Monteiro. ABOVE: *Outcroppings of rock and free-form areas of plantings create asymmetrical harmony.*

ABOVE: *A sunny profusion of day lilies, accented by sculptural cactus forms, exemplifies Senhor Burle Marx's use of indigenous plants to blend the garden with its environment.* RIGHT: *An accomplished painter, Roberto Burle Marx approaches landscape design as a work of art, thinking in terms of dimension and volume. A footpath, which winds through the entire garden, illustrates his concept by threading past a sequence of large and small, dense and widespread plantings. Skirting the pond created for the garden, it branches off to become a bridge of stepping-stones.*

TOP AND OPPOSITE: *At the far end of the garden rises a steep mountain, whose familiar shape inspires friends to say Odette Monteiro has her own private Sugar Loaf. The pond provides the focus of the landscape.*

ABOVE LEFT: *A low swath of coleus, used as a ground cover, bands a grove of trees stippled with bougainvillea.*
ABOVE RIGHT: *Spiky plant forms give definition to a patch of rock garden.*

Thomas Edison's Botanical Garden

The Moreton Bay Fig, which Edison brought back from Australia, was a potential source of rubber.

BEHIND A PICKET fence and a high hedge, tropical plants flourish in the fourteen-acre garden surrounding Thomas Edison's former winter home in Fort Myers, Florida. The warm, moist air is filled with mysterious fragrances and, rooted high on bark and branches, epiphytic plants flaunt their exotic forms. Beauty prevails, although it was scientific experimentation that led Edison to assemble this extraordinary collection of more than 600 botanical species.

The inventor was thirty-eight when he first came to Fort Myers in the winter of 1884–1885, in search of a new home. Exhausted by his arduous working habits, recently widowed and with three young children to care for, he had been warned by his doctors that if he expected to live he must seek a warmer climate and spend more time outdoors. Exploring the Caloosahatchee River by boat, he was drawn to a spot where a magnificent stand of wild bamboo grew at the water's edge. The following winter he returned with his bride, Mina Miller, and the adventurous couple set about planning their permanent winter home and garden.

Mrs. Edison, who was an avid gardener, envisioned a genteel estate with tidy flower beds and a wide lawn sweeping down to the river. But Edison, whose hobby was botany and horticulture, could not resist planting every open space with experimental specimens— each a source of a product or by-product that might be useful in one of his inventions. Seeking a filament for his most famous one, the electric light bulb, he discovered that bamboo fibers outlasted every other organic substance. He eventually tested 6,000 plants, finally deciding on a common Japanese variety, *Bambusa argentea*. Many other specimens were planted as he sought a natural source of rubber, foreseeing the day when international problems might cut off foreign supplies. Edison designed Florida's first modern swimming pool, using Edison Portland Cement, another of his discoveries.

His health improved by his garden, Thomas Edison lived to age eighty-four. It has been calculated that during a thirty-year period he patented a new invention every ten days. Add to this the number of tropical plant specimens he introduced to the United States, and his achievements appear still more astounding. His vast legacy of new inventions enriched humanity beyond measure, changing forever the technologies of mankind.

A tropical garden filled with more than 600 plant species surrounds Thomas Edison's former winter home in Fort Myers, Florida. The inventor favored plants that were useful for their products and by-products. For many years, the boat dock provided the only access to the property.

LEFT: *Vines cascade over a small laboratory/office set within a secluded garden area featuring a sunken pool.* ABOVE: *The Natal plum, an ornamental shrub, bears fragrant blossoms as well as edible fruit.*

Foreseeing a time when the United States would be cut off from its foreign supply, Edison and his friends Henry Ford and Harvey Firestone sought a natural source of rubber that could be grown domestically. In his quest the inventor planted a banyan tree that Mr. Firestone brought back from India as a four-foot seedling in 1925.

ABOVE AND RIGHT: *The serpentine roots of the Moreton Bay fig extend 200 feet from the trunk of the tree.*

A Desert Haven
under the Arizona Sun

The cow-tongue prickly pear.

"I AM A MAN of the desert," said the late John Rhuart. "I think best when I'm walking through my garden. I pull a forgotten weed now and then; I listen to the cooing of the mourning doves. It is a sort of meditation, a communion with nature. Here in Phoenix, the air feels best very early in the morning; the desert is still cool, the flowers fresh and dewy. The heat is not yet oppressive, but in any case I have become quite accustomed to it."

After living for fifty years in his Phoenix home, Mr. Rhuart moved to the nearby slopes of Camelback Mountain twenty-two years ago. Shaped as its name suggests, Camelback abounds with cactus and sagebrush, and Mr. Rhuart chose his site primarily for its landscape possibilities. The property encompasses a small hill between two dry gullies. Mr. Rhuart built the house on top of the hill, the pool at the bottom, in the hollow. A terraced garden of brilliant color completes the setting.

The landscaping and terracing of the three-acre garden took three years to complete. "I was one of the first to buy property in this area," John Rhuart said, "so I had to build a road to bring the palm trees from the old house. Thirty-six trees, up to a hundred feet tall and weighing as much as nine tons each, were transported on extra-long flatbed trailers to the site, where a crane lowered them into the ground." Surrounding the mosaic pool, the towering one-hundred-foot palm trees, now over seventy years old, seem all the more impressive for the Herculean undertaking.

The sparse desert earth of Camelback Mountain is primarily decomposed granite, and each year Mr. Rhuart brought in tons of new garden soil to replace what had been washed away by the rains and the watering. "When the planting season begins, in October," he explained, "we put in bulbs from Holland and seeds from various places in the world. We continue planting through the year: daffodils, tulips, hyacinths, which bloom in February, ranunculuses, which flower in March, zinnias and daisies in the summer."

John Rhuart was truly at peace in this environment. The setting sun etches the skeleton of a giant saguaro cactus against the darkening sky, and jackrabbits hop past the foot of a monstrous elephant cactus. In the still, dry air, the surrealistic mood of the landscape never lost its allure for this man of the desert.

The late John Rhuart was inextricably linked to Phoenix, Arizona, and two of the city's exceptional desert oases flourished under his care. As founder of the 150-acre Desert Botanical Garden, he was knowledgeable about a host of cactus species, including the totem pole cactus, above. His home, Palmas Altas, took its name from the stately palms growing there.

ABOVE: *The tangled chain-fruit cholla has a characteristically descriptive name.* RIGHT: *The organ-pipe cactus is a fine upstanding presence in a rock garden colored by nasturtiums and African daisies.* OPPOSITE: *Beside the slender aloe, the elephant cactus, which can weigh more than ten tons, is truly the desert's mammoth.*

ABOVE: *Mexican fan palms and century plants stand guard while ranunculuses, gazanias and petunias bloom on the terraced desert hillside at Palmas Altas.* LEFT: *The hedgehog cactus illustrates the aptness of the names given to many desert-loving species.*

155

Haus zur Palme near Zurich

A handsome pair of hyacinth macaws, devoted mates, enjoy a moment's rest in their garden habitat.

T UCKED AWAY in the countryside a few miles from Zurich lies a garden filled with tropical plants and colorfully plumed exotic birds. From early spring until autumn, flowers of many hues fill the air with perfume. This unique and unexpected location is the creation of Peter Buhofer, who, when gardening as a hobby ceased to satisfy him, gave up his Zurich antiques gallery, purchased a house in the country, and began another chapter in his varied history.

To find plants for his garden, Mr. Buhofer made forays into tropical lands, studying and collecting specimens as he went. He began his odyssey in the Caribbean, continued his travels to South and Central America, and then went on to Thailand, Cambodia and Vietnam. Later, he visited southern California and Hawaii. As Switzerland does not ban the importation of plants, the only real difficulty he faced was keeping his finds alive during the trip home.

At *Haus zur Palme*, "most of the plants go into the greenhouses before the first frost comes," Mr. Buhofer explains. "This usually occurs at the end of October, and at that time they must be moved rather quickly. Most of them are put outside again around the end of April. The Swiss climate is conducive to good plant health because there is lots of rain and a humid atmosphere."

Mr. Buhofer's interest in tropical birds grew apace with his enthusiasm for tropical plants. He acquired his first bird, José, thirty years ago in Central Africa. The only talking bird in the garden, José's repertoire includes the entire melody of the march from *The Bridge on the River Kwai*. In fine weather the birds are free to roam about the grounds. The larger ones—among them a pair of crowned cranes from Africa—occupy a pond in an enclosure behind the house. So well have they adapted to the Swiss climate that they have even developed a love for snow. Two Swiss geese serve as watchdogs, making a frightful clamor whenever a marauding fox appears.

The garden, with its many birds and great variety of plants, is a demanding commitment. A rainstorm can reduce it to a shambles, while a few dry days can endanger the very lives of some plants. There are no dull moments. But the beauty that rewards constant experimentation and care is everywhere apparent in this Arcadian landscape, which Peter Buhofer describes with a sincere fondness as his "delightful little jungle."

Peter Buhofer defied climate to establish a miniature jungle in the countryside near Zurich. The brilliant macaws are among the smaller birds inhabiting the garden. They pass most warm-weather days outside their cages, perched picturesquely on chairs and tables or in convenient treetops.

Day lilies, a tobacco plant, mallow and an angel trumpet tree flourish in the moist pseudo-tropical poolside environment.

Serving as a living room in summer, the Greenhouse shelters the tender plants throughout the cold winters. *Reflected sunlight streaks the azure pool, like lightning bolts transfixed in a foreign medium.*

158

Alfresco dining is enhanced by a view of a crystal-clear pool surrounded by lush verdure. "The Swiss climate is conducive to good plant health, because there's lots of rain and a humid atmosphere," says Peter Buhofer.

ABOVE AND RIGHT: *Foliage is particularly dense around a water-lily pond, where fish and frogs make their home.*

OPPOSITE: *Most debonair is the regal crowned crane, who lives happily with several varieties of ducks and geese. While many of the larger birds originally came from the tropics, their adaptation has been so complete that they remain outdoors even in winter.*

Tresco Abbey off Lands End

Wild ferns and rocky outcrops fringe Abbey Pool, a lush haven for migratory seabirds.

T WENTY-EIGHT miles southwest of Lands End, England, on a rugged island barely two miles long and one mile wide, lies a subtropical garden filled with exotic plants. Tresco Abbey Gardens is the private estate of a family that for four generations has governed Tresco, one of the five inhabited Isles of Scilly. The residents live in quaint stone cottages, each with its flower garden. But the real splendor of the island is the twelve-acre Abbey House garden.

A monument to Neptune crowns the highest point. Gazing over tall palms and billowing flame trees, the stone bust surveys the garden and, beyond it, the blue Atlantic. A maze of footpaths and rough-hewn stone steps interlaces the garden's three main levels. Lighthouse Walk, a narrow avenue of tall hedges and palm trees, bisects the grounds, joining the terraces with stone steps that begin at an old lighthouse lantern and lead up to the bust of Neptune.

Near the house stand the remains of a tenth-century Benedictine monastery—a stone wall and archway where flowering vines, succulents and hanging plants flourish. The monastery had long since fallen to ruin when, in 1834, Augustus Smith, first lord proprietor of the Scillies, arrived. A wealthy landowner from the mainland, Smith was in quest of an isolated spot where he could implement his political beliefs. The Scillies were impoverished and ripe for reform.

Not a single tree grew on the wind-thrashed archipelago, yet their potential was great. For between ferocious storms, the islands, warmed by the Gulf Stream, are blessed with a delightful climate: Their beaches are powder white, their waters the clearest blue, and their winters balmy. Under Smith's rule, the islanders quickly became industrious shipbuilders and skillful farmers. Many rose to be sea captains, returning from their voyages bearing rare and exotic plants, and these specimens found a home in the rapidly growing garden surrounding Smith's residence.

Robert A. Dorrien Smith, a descendant of the first governor, now lives on the estate with his wife, Emma, and their son, Adam. The young couple are determined to preserve the unique character of the island and hope to expand further their already vast plant collection. As long as Neptune keeps watch, the garden will remain a lush Hesperides of perpetual summertime, sunshine and flowers.

Powdery beaches and clear blue water rim the tiny island of Tresco, one of the Isles of Scilly, 28 miles from Lands End, England. Augustus Smith, first lord proprietor of the Scillies, settled on the island in 1834 and transformed the barren, wind-thrashed spot into an Eden. Four generations of Smiths have lived here.

ABOVE: *A myriad of plants co-exist in a bounty of subtropical forms.*

RIGHT AND FAR RIGHT: *Hardy ice plants hide a rock in a blaze of color, while other flowering succulents run riot among the boulders.*

Plants decorate a cliffside where a century and a half ago granite blocks were quarried for building the residence. The dense screen of hedges softens the impact of Atlantic gales that frequently tear across the island.

An arch overgrown with vines and flowering rock plants is all that remains of a Benedictine monastery founded on the site of the garden in the 10th century.

ABOVE: *Nature takes poetic license, mingling nemesia, campanula and sweet peas, to describe one of many small, secluded glades.*

RIGHT: *A rocky embankment borders a section in the maze of footpaths and stone stairways that link the garden's three main levels.*

FAR RIGHT: *The view from the terrace of Tresco Abbey House culminates in the neighboring island of St. Mary's.*

The Tahitian Paradise
of Motu Ovini

A pond is surrounded by lush growth.

O N APRIL 11, 1776, the *Endeavor* sighted the peaks of Tahiti. The ship's naturalist, Parkinson, was moved to write: "The land appeared as uneven as a piece of crumpled paper, being divided irregularly into hills and valleys, but a beautiful verdure covered both, even to the tops of the highest peaks." That, too, is how Tahiti must have appeared to Harrison Willard Smith on his first visit to the island, in 1903. Born in Boston thirty-one years before, he taught physics at a university in Cambridge, Massachusetts. When he saw Tahiti, a long-time interest in tropical and exotic flora became more than a hobby—it became his life's work.

In 1919 Smith moved permanently to Tahiti with the intention of organizing a garden where he could grow tropical plants. At that time he inherited a considerable fortune, a circumstance that allowed him to abandon his other professional activities and dedicate his life to the creation of the garden. Like Gauguin, who had visited the area before him, Smith was enchanted by the rustic village of Papeari, fifty kilometers from Papeete: "It has a calm, end-of-the-world quality, far away from the bustle of Papeete." Towering *mape*, the Tahitian chestnut trees, grow thick along the Vaite, the small river that maintains the humidity around their tortured roots. Smith chose three small valleys, comprising 274 acres, to become the estate of *Motu Ovini*.

It is impossible today to evaluate the gift of beauty that Smith gave Tahiti, on which there is a surprising scarcity of native flora. In all, he introduced 250 new species that are both useful and a pleasure to see. He traveled extensively to collect new specimens: in 1921 to Sarawak, Singapore, Trinidad and Cuba; later, to Java, Ceylon, Hawaii and Rabaul. Smith also kept up an unceasing correspondence with specialists in tropical gardens of Southeast Asia and the New World, and from these sources enriched his collections immeasurably.

In the end, Harrison Willard Smith, who died in Papeari in 1947, was a great public benefactor. He gave plants and seeds to those who asked for them; he went to people's homes to graft specimens; he organized contests for the most beautiful gardens and flowers. Today Papeari remains the flower district of Tahiti, and the Smith gardens surround the Gauguin Museum, a memorial to another for whom this Polynesian isle became both home and inspiration.

Bostonian Harrison Smith began forming the Motu Ovini estate in 1919. He was known as "Grandfather of the Trees" because of the 250 botanical species he brought to Tahiti. In a coconut grove along the lagoon, a hibiscus sheds its blossoms.

ABOVE: *A stream running through the golf course at Atimaono, on the site of a former sugar cane plantation, is bordered by cannas, widely used in Tahitian gardens. The flowers of the fragrant plumeria trees are used in the making of leis.* RIGHT: *A young bamboo contrasts with older stalks that have become encrusted with lichens.*

TOP: *A pond bordered by a palm-studded meadow marks one of the varied areas of Motu Ovini, an estate of almost 300 acres.* ABOVE: *An aquatic scene at the Millaud Gardens, the land that adjoins Motu Ovini, in the village of Mataiea, shows a tropical abundance of water lilies, cannas and weeping willows.*

OPPOSITE: *Overlooking a boxwood maze, a topiary camel, of privet, needs water far more often than its animal counterpart.* ABOVE: *Gardener George Mendonca uses four shrubs to create quadrupeds, like the mountain goat. Starting with the first new leaves of spring, he trims the garden's privet and boxwood figures every two to four weeks, depending upon the amount of rain and resulting growth spurts.*

The Ohme Gardens in the Wenatchee Valley

Basket-of-gold brightens a small knoll.

P ERCHED HIGH on a rocky bluff overlooking the Wenatchee Valley
in central Washington, *Ohme Gardens* combine the lush growth
of a rain forest, the variegated patterns of an Alpine meadow and the
richly colored hues of an artist's palette. Ground-hugging plants surround small pools, rustic shelters, secluded hideaways and patches
of velvety green lawn. Native-stone pathways lead from one level to
another among weathered rock outcroppings thrust up through
carpetlike plantings. Below, the Columbia River cuts a blue swath
through the fertile valley; in the distance loom the Cascades, whose
rugged beauty inspired the creation of the gardens—on a small
mountainside of their own—over fifty years ago.

From the beginning, the Ohme Gardens were a family collaboration. In 1929, Herman Ohme and his bride, Ruth, acquired forty
acres of land for fruit orchards. Included was a craggy, rock-strewn
bluff. Dry and desolate, its only vegetation was a scattering of desert
sage. Yet the grandeur of the setting enabled the young couple to
envision their future garden on this arid spot.

Together the Ohmes would drive into the mountains and return
home with the rumble seat of their automobile laden with small
evergreen trees. They planted the saplings among the bluff's boulders and nourished them with water from the valley below. They
hauled native stones to form trails and borders. They removed desert sage and replaced it with low-growing ground covers. With the
help of a mule and a drag bucket, they carved out a pool against a
massive rock formation. Little by little the Ohmes transformed the
dry hill, and blended together trees, low-growing plants, water and
stone to make a landscape so natural in appearance that it seems to
have been this way always. Actually, it took more than a thousand
transplanted trees to produce this seemingly spontaneous effect.

Having begun the gardens when they were first married, Herman and Ruth Ohme shared their dream for forty-two years, until
1971, when Mr. Ohme died at the age of eighty. Ruth Ohme contin-
ues to help in the gardens, now principally the responsibility of her
son Gordon. Through his efforts, they have nearly doubled in size,
to their present nine acres. He and his wife, Carol, have three young
sons, and all do their part. Indeed, it is likely that for many years
wasteland will be infused with beauty by the hand of an Ohme.

In 1929, inspired by the beauty of the nearby Cascade Mountains, Herman and Ruth Ohme decided to create a garden on their own small mountain overlooking Washington's Wenatchee Valley. Their son Gordon now carries on the tradition. The hidden pool area reveals the blending of water, trees, and stone.

OPPOSITE: *Fir trees and ground covers contribute color and softness—and stop erosion of the rugged terrain.* ABOVE: *In the central garden, trees delicately shade an idyllic sylvan pool, a special retreat that rewards the Ohmes' efforts. Water —pumped up the bluff from the valley below—is just one of the gardens' essential ingredients. Needed to supply pools, streams and waterfalls, it is also necessary for extensive irrigation.* LEFT: *Crowning a view point, a drift of candytuft imitates clouds over nearby mountains.*

LEFT: *Phlox and basket-of-gold manage to take hold even in the rockiest parts of the gardens, where sunlight seems to carve shadows into stone. Most of the plants can survive with very little soil, provided they get ample water.* BELOW: *Winding against a parade of fir trees, a small path leads toward the hidden pool, in the lower reaches of the garden. Pathways and steps, built of native stone and integrated with the existing rock formations, enhance the garden's natural appearance.*

OPPOSITE: *Modeled after high mountain country, the latest major addition to the gardens is the twin pools area, which was completed in 1972. The lower pool is fed by a little stream running from the smaller one above it. Dianthus, thyme and goldmoss sedum blanket the rock-studded mountainside.* FOLLOWING PAGES: *The gardens—intended as a small sanctuary—have progressed from rock-strewn desolation to nine acres of lush and colorful splendor.*

A Garden of Stone Monsters North of Rome

The bearded figure may be Neptune or a river god.

A T THE FOOT of a towering crag on which perches the Medieval hamlet of Bomarzo, some fifty miles north of Rome, lies *The Garden of Monsters*. An assortment of sculptured stone figures, some of them horrendous, the statues are all that remain of a sixteenth-century enigma that has never been solved. A first impression of the garden is blandly deceptive. Through the charming gate of crenellated stone, a small sphinx smiles coyly. A path ascends a knoll at whose summit stands a pseudo-Palladian Temple of Love. A myriad species of trees surround a lush meadow where flights of moss-covered stone steps follow the rolling terrain.

Then, without warning, there looms a monster, much too close for comfort—an enormous ogre's mask with bulging eyes and gaping mouth. Its powerful jaws seem ready to clamp down on any mortal so foolish as to come within their range. A few feet farther on, a life-size figure of an elephant carries on its back a female figure, and in its trunk that of a male, which, on examination, it seems to be strangling. Nearby, a ferocious dragon battles a lioness for possession of the latter's cubs.

Hoping to uncover the garden's beginnings, Prince Giovanni Borghese, whose family has owned the property since 1836 and who played here as a child, delved into his family archives. Bomarzo's history, he says, goes back to the Etruscans, who were followed by the Romans. In 1502 Prince Corrado Orsini, whose family held power in Italy for five centuries, took possession of the hamlet of Bomarzo and converted the local fortress into a castle. His son Vicino created the present garden sometime in the latter half of the sixteenth century, yet the name of the sculptor still defies discovery.

One theory holds that Prince Vicino worked along with artists he hired to make the figures. Prince Borghese, however, thinks the garden was peopled with grotesques long before the Orsini came to Bomarzo. Legend tells of an earthquake centuries before, and he thinks this is when the stones from which the statues were carved— at a much later date—fell into the valley. Still more tales abound: of Turkish prisoners of war and of Persians who, some say, sculpted the monsters. Whatever the truth may be, Prince Vicino Orsini succeeded in producing a unique assemblage of art and horror, mystifying all who have seen it over the years.

Mystery surrounds the 16th-century origins of the Garden of Monsters, in the tiny Italian village of Bomarzo—and little is known of the sculptors who created the stone figures inhabiting it. ABOVE: *An ogre's mask may symbolize the entrance to the river Styx. The words carved around the mouth mean "Every thought takes flight."*

Coming upon the garden in 1950, Salvador Dali prompted Prince Giovanni Borghese—whose family acquired the property in 1836—to investigate its origins. The prince found that Prince Vicino Orsini had created it in the latter part of the 16th century.

LEFT: *An elephant, carrying a female figure and a castle-shaped howdah, towers 16 feet high.* BELOW LEFT: *A pair of lions guard a poetic winged mermaid.* BELOW RIGHT: *A goddess balances a plant-filled urn atop her head.* OPPOSITE: *A lioness bravely defends her cubs against an attacking dragon. All of the figures are approximately twice life-size.*

The Duke Gardens of Somerville

The marble statue Majesty *rises from a bed of tulips in the French Garden.*

INSIDE THE Duke Gardens at Somerville, New Jersey, eleven spacious, luxurious greenhouses reflect the gardening traditions of different civilizations, periods and parts of the world. The gardens, open to the public ten months each year, are the property of the Duke Gardens Foundation. Miss Doris Duke, who inherited *Duke Farms* from her father, made a gift of the greenhouses to the foundation when it was incorporated in 1958. She has been primarily responsible for the gardens: designing their layout, finding the suitable plant material, supervising their planting and maintenance.

Visitors first encounter the *Italian Garden*, a re-creation of those seen by late-eighteenth-century Europeans on the Grand Tour. Next is the *Colonial Garden*, where camellias, oleanders, *Magnolia grandiflora* and crape myrtle induce a perceptible Southern ambience. The adjoining *Edwardian Garden* is presented as a greenhouse—a conservatory of the type in vogue among wealthy English and Americans during the closing years of the nineteenth century. In the *French Garden*, plantings of chrysanthemums, tulips, primroses and petunias succeed one another, as the months go by, in an intricate maze of clipped ilex and boxwood edging. The neighboring *English Garden* displays lawns of spotless velvet green, and flowers mingle indiscriminately in long herbaceous borders.

After these, the *Desert Garden* comes as a shock—all rock, soil and cactus, aloe and prickly pear—like a remote corner of the American Southwest. Next come two Far Eastern gardens. In the *Chinese Garden*, bold rock formations and free-growing shrubs stimulate and refresh the imagination, while the *Japanese Garden* is designed for meditation. Inside the *Indo-Persian Garden*, brick paths on either side of running water reproduce in miniature one of the features of the Shalimar Gardens in Lahore. From this delicate beauty, visitors plunge into the *Tropical Garden*, a rain forest where fronds shut out the sky and lesser foliage clusters around a stream and waterfall. Then on to the *Semi-tropical Garden*, an evocation of gardens enjoyed by Spanish colonists in California and Latin America.

Each garden evokes the ambience of a location, a period, a culture. Doris Duke's transformation of Duke Farms into this unique display is truly a gift to every person who sees them.

*At the Duke Gardens in Somerville, New Jersey, under the loving guidance of
Miss Doris Duke, each of eleven greenhouses has been designed to represent a
microcosm of one of the world's horticultural traditions.* ABOVE: *In the Indo-Persian
Garden, clipped blue Italian cypress and citrus trees parallel the brickwork.*

LEFT: *The Tropical Garden, a miniature rain forest, is shadowy with ferns, bromeliads and dracaena.* BELOW: *A door, made on the premises in the manner of classic French latticework, opens to a garden beyond.*

LEFT: *After the style popular during the reign of Louis XVI, the French Garden contains a parterre, with shapes outlined by English boxwood and English and Japanese holly. Ivy on the columns was bred on the estate for leaves with especially long points.*

In the traditional Chinese Garden, evocative rock formations and luxuriant plants fulfill their purpose—to offer the imagination free rein. ABOVE: Black bamboo, believed to give protection, weeping willow and jasmine surround a miniature "Island of the Immortals," dedicated to ancestors. RIGHT: The summerhouse shadows a growth of white pine.

BELOW: *A path, zigzagged in characteristic Chinese fashion to delude evil spirits, leads to the Moon Gate.* LEFT: *Through the Moon Gate, the lattice courtyard, of hand-tied bamboo, provides a setting for a variety of bonsai trees.*

OPPOSITE: *Hinting at onetime formality, a limestone sculpture, The Three Graces, is partly obscured by oleander and bougainvillea, growing at will. Swedish ivy embraces the fountain.*

The Italian Garden reflects the late-18th-century admiration for classic order, softened by the passage of time. ABOVE: *Apparently abandoned to nature's whim, a limestone sculpture against an acacia reflects post-Renaissance Italian landscapes.* RIGHT: *In spring, daffodils replace the begonias at the Entrance to the gardens. At other times, clivia, marigolds, impatiens and orchids vie for this choice spot.*

The Enchanting Ninfa Gardens in Italy

An ancient moss-covered bridge spans the River Ninfa.

NINFA LIES in a marshy valley known as the Agro Pontino, about sixty-eight kilometers south of Rome. The region was already settled in prehistoric times, and overlooking Ninfa are the remains of Stone Age constructions. By the Middle Ages the area was a large farm, given by Emperor Constantine to Pope Zacharias. Under the Church's protection it flourished, and the city of Ninfa sprang up. A convenient stopping point on the Appian Way, it acquired great importance, but its reputation attracted covetous Roman barons, who wrested it from the Church.

Once the stronghold of the noble Frangipani family, then of the powerful Caetani counts, and finally of the Borgias, Ninfa was abandoned in the middle of the fifteenth century, unable to withstand the twin calamities of civil war and malaria. Untouched for centuries, the marshes were drained about 1930 and the Caetani family—including three horticulturists—reestablished the gardens.

Serving as a visual counterpoint to the vigor and lushness of the plantings stand the ruins of the Caetani castle, with its high crenellated tower, and of the cathedral of Santa Maria Maggiore, in which Pope Alexander III was crowned. Through the grounds flows the river that takes its name from the Italian word for nymph—*ninfa*—chosen, history records, because in Roman times a temple to the nymphs stood nearby. Several bridges cross the river, the oldest of which, the Ponte Marcello, is a graceful arch of moss-covered stone.

Each year, the first blossoms to appear are those of flowering trees: Japanese cherry, plum, peach and crab apple, whose blossoms tint the landscape with delicate hues. Tulip trees and white snowball bushes enhance this subtle palette. Lining the banks of streams are dense stands of calla lilies. Beside a pond, a vivid show of Japanese irises mingles with the reeds; by another, sunny irises glow. An enormous parasol made entirely of softly shaded tea roses stands as a living monument to a gardener's expertise.

Masses of roses, climbing over the ruins of this once proud imperial fiefdom, seem a particularly appropriate flower for the gardens of Ninfa. As stately as the city may have been, little remains; but the gardens of Ninfa are a tribute to the noble family that rescued the neglected land, and a reminder that while what man builds is transitory, the beauties of nature are eternal.

The ruins of a Medieval walled city lend an enchanted atmosphere to the luxuriant Ninfa Gardens in Italy's fertile Agro Pontino Valley. ABOVE: *An unruffled lake reflects billowy clouds and the crenellated tower of the castle built by Pietro Caetani during the Middle Ages, around 1300.*

The gardens, set in the tree-stippled foothills of the Appenines, abound with water welling up from underground. LEFT: *Near a gate leading to the tower is a small pond, fed by a waterfall and bracketed by beds of irises.* ABOVE: *A second pond, ringed with calla lilies, ripples past stately cypress trees, orderly hedges, colorful rosebushes and the crumbling remains of another tower.*

ABOVE: *Fragrant rows of lavender bushes, the cascading blooms of a cherry tree and crumbling masonry punctuate the garden's daisy-studded lawn.* LEFT: *Proclaiming the spring, crab apple trees in full flower tint the sky with blossoms.*

OPPOSITE: *The ever-present confluence of water, stone and flowers endows the gardens with multifaceted beauty. A pine shades a lily-bordered bank of the Ninfa.*

Deerfield Maze
near Philadelphia

*The stone and plaster springhouse
nestles in a sheltered glen.*

THE FRAGRANCE of English boxwood pervades the air. at *Deer-field*, the forty-five-acre Pennsylvania estate of Mr. and Mrs. H. Thomas Hallowell, Jr. Colorful azalea beds, fine stands of trees and luxuriant lawns surround the pride of the garden, a formal maze nurtured from seedlings since 1947, when the Hallowells acquired what was then an old farmstead.

"When we purchased the property, we inherited the services of an elderly farmhand who lived here with his family," says Mr. Hallowell, "and to keep him busy we decided to cultivate the garden. I began by purchasing 10,000 azalea cuttings from a mail-order catalogue." Transforming barren fields into great sweeps of lawn, he relieved their uniformity with azalea beds of every shape and color.

Shortly afterward, 3,500 English boxwood plants were offered by a local nursery. Mr. Hallowell purchased the lot and planted them in hedges and avenues—straight lines that divide the garden into sections, and gentle curves that follow the contour of a slope or a winding path. But the boxwood nursery was still quite full when he read about the famous maze in the gardens of England's Hampton Court Palace. "We had visited Hampton Court a few years earlier, and had gotten ourselves lost in the maze, so we were thoroughly familiar with the overall design," says Mr. Hallowell. "In a flash of inspiration we realized what a splendid maze we could create with our own English boxwood, and we immediately set to work on a half-size replica of the Hampton Court maze."

Situated at the edge of a rectangular lawn, the maze at Deerfield is flanked on three sides by azalea borders. In spring, the bright new growth of the boxwood and the strict geometry of the maze make a bold contrast to the vivid colors of the azaleas. Strategically placed among them, white and pink flowering dogwood, Japanese andromeda, native American rhododendron and mountain laurel intensify the dazzling profusion of colors and delicate fragrances.

Mr. and Mrs. Hallowell, often accompanied by their dogs, enjoy nothing better than strolling through the garden they have nurtured for so long. The vast stretches of lawn are laced with a hundred different kinds of trees and 5,000 feet of boxwood hedge. Walking trails crisscross deciduous woods populated with ancient trees. After thirty-six years, Deerfield has never looked lovelier.

In the 36 years since Mr. and Mrs. H. Thomas Hallowell, Jr. acquired Deerfield, in Rydal, Pennsylvania, they have transformed it from a simple farmstead into a lushly planted parkland. ABOVE: *A horticultural tour de force, the boxwood maze was shaped from numerous seedlings. Its height reflects long years of nurturing.*

Cradled at the bottom of a valley, Deerfield's lake empties over a stone spillway vaulted by a Japanese-inspired humpback bridge. A pair of Canada geese have claimed the lake as their domain, much to the pleasure of the Hallowells.

Ostrich ferns and brilliant azaleas surround the stone and plaster springhouse. The spontaneous pattern of color is the fortuitous result of Mr. Hallowell's hastening to rescue the azalea seedlings from overcrowding in their nursery beds.

ABOVE: *Behind a mass of azaleas rises
a reminder of the original farmstead;
buildings on the property include a barn,
corncrib and stable, and the residence, a
stout stone farmhouse built in 1804.*

LEFT: *Inspired by their visits to the
maze at Hampton Court Palace in
England, and its replica at the Governor's Palace in Colonial Williamsburg,
the Hallowells decided to create their
own half-size version of that design. It
happily resolved the question of what to
do with the better part of 3,500 English
boxwood plants they had recently
purchased from a local nursery.*

Credits and Acknowledgments

The Knapp Press is a wholly owned subsidiary of Knapp Communications Corporation
Chairman and Chief Executive Officer: Cleon T. Knapp
President: H. Stephen Cranston
Senior Vice-Presidents: Paige Rense (Editor-in-Chief), Everett T. Alcan (Corporate Planning), Rosalie Bruno (New Venture Development), Harry Myers (Magazine Group Publisher), Betsy Wood Knapp (MIS Electronic Media), L. James Wade, Jr. (Finance)

The Knapp Press
President: Alice Bandy; Administrative Assistant: Beth Bell; Senior Editor: Norman Kolpas; Associate Editors: Jeff Book, Jan Koot, Sarah Lifton, Pamela Mosher; Editor, Gault Millau: Deborah Patton; Assistant Editors: Taryn Bigelow, Colleen Dunn, Jan Stuebing; Editorial Assistant: Nancy D. Roberts; Art Director: Paula Schlosser; Designers: Robin Murawski, Nan Oshin; Book Production Manager: Larry Cooke; Production Coordinator: Joan Valentine; Managing Director, Rosebud Books: Robert Groag; Financial Analyst: Carlton Joseph; Assistant Finance Manager: Kerri Culbertson; Fulfillment Services Manager: Virginia Parry; Director of Public Relations: Jan B. Fox; Promotions Manager: Jeanie Gould; Promotions Coordinator: Joanne Denison; Marketing Assistant: Dolores Briqueleur; Special Sales: Lynn Blocker; Department Secretaries: Amy Hershman, Randy Levin

We would also like to acknowledge Patrick R. Casey, Vice-President, Production, Knapp Communications Corporation; Anthony P. Iacono, Vice-President, Manufacturing, Knapp Communications Corporation; Philip Kaplan, Vice-President, Graphics, Knapp Communications Corporation; Donna Clipperton, Manager, Rights and Permissions, Knapp Communications Corporation and Faith Haase, Rights and Permissions Coordinator, Knapp Communications Corporation.

Writers

The following writers prepared the original *Architectural Digest* articles from which the material in this book has been adapted:

Sir Harold Acton
Helen Barnes
Katia Bojilova-Beebe
Allen Carter
Barnaby Conrad
Dorothy Young Croman
Derek Fell
David Halliday
Hathaway Hardy
Joanne Jaffe
Maggie Keswick
Elizabeth Lambert
Valentine Lawford
Christopher Lloyd
Nigel Nicolson
Elizabeth Sault
Elaine B. Steiner

All original text adapted by Cameron Curtis McKinley

All original captions adapted by Mary Chesterfield and Joanne Jaffe

Chapter introductions by Elizabeth Lambert

Special thanks to Georgia Griggs and Bernice Lifton

Photographers

Timothy Beddow *116–123*
Morton Beebe *130, 132–137, 150–155, 168–171*
Robert Emmett Bright *30, 32–43, 156–161, 186–189, 198–203*
Dick Busher *178–185*
Allen Carter *138–143*
Richard Champion *104–109, 172, 174–177, 190–197*
Bruno de Hamel *14–19, 20–23*
Derek Fell *2, 10–13, 52–57, 65, 68–71, 78–89, 90–96, 98–103, 110–115, 124–129, 144–149, 162–167, 204–209*
Marie Holstein *72–77*
Derry Moore *4–9, 24–29*
J. Barry O'Rourke *62, 64, 66–67*
Naoyuki Shimizu *46–51*
Herman How-Man Wong *44, 58–61*

Design

Book and jacket design by Paula Schlosser

Page layout by Nan Oshin
Mechanicals by Betty Shimotsuka

This book is set in Bembo. Composition was on the Merganthaler Linotron 202 by Graphic Typesetting Service

Text stock: Mead Web Gloss, basis 80

Color separation and film work by Liberty Photo Engraving Company

Printing and binding by W.A. Krueger